# The Raven and the Writing-Desk

# Francis Huxley

# The Raven
## and the
# Writing
# Desk

Harper & Row, Publishers
New York, Hagerstown, San Francisco, London

'However, I'll consider if I will or not — meanwhile I send a little thing to give you
an idea of what I look like when I'm lecturing. The merest sketch, you will allow
— yet still I think there's something grand in the expression of the brow and in the
action of the hand.' (Letter to Maggie Cunningham, Jan 30 1868.)

FIRST U.S. EDITION

ISBN: 0-06-012113-0

LIBRARY OF CONGRESS CATALOG CARD NUMBER: 75-30333

# Contents

# A very old explanation

The title of this enquiry comes, as all readers of *Alice's Adventures in Wonderland* will know, from the famous riddle that the Hatter put to Alice at the start of the Mad Tea-party. It is famous because, when she asked the Hatter 'What's the answer?' he replied that he had not the slightest idea. This provoked her weary comment that he might do something better with the time than waste it asking riddles with no answers – as well he might have, since by age-old tradition a riddle with no answer is dangerous nonsense, the forfeit for asking it being to lose your head.

Of course, the Hatter never *said* it was a riddle when he asked it, so the charge that it is nonsense must fail. ('"You may go," said the King, and the Hatter hurriedly left the court, without even waiting to put his shoes on.') To make the charge stick we must give nonsense a capital, as Carroll himself sometimes did, and call it Nonsense. ('" – and just take his head off outside," the Queen added to one of the officers.') Since he did the same to the Hatter's riddle, we shall follow suit and call it the Riddle. These are simple enough changes but, as may already be suspected, they lead directly to some hair-raising matters. We shall hunt them down in good time, following Carroll's lead; but here we may usefully refer to the dictionary as one way of keeping our bearings. There, under 'capital', we find the entry: 'relating to the head: involving the death penalty: placed at the head: ... a large letter ...: the stock of money used for carrying on any business...' (*Chambers's Twentieth Century Dictionary*.)

What has all this to do with the Riddle? Why, it was the Hatter who asked it. What is our justification for dragging in these puns by their heels? We shall find it if we can make capital of two lines from Carroll's 'Phantasmagoria' (1869):

> '"The man", says Johnson, "that would make
> A pun, would pick a pocket!"'

Indeed he would. For if we return to the Tea-party that is endlessly taking place in front of the March Hare's house, we shall find that a silence fell over the company soon after the Riddle had been asked. The Hatter then took a watch out of his pocket, and asked what day of the month it was. Since his watch was two days wrong,

7

*Alice Liddell, photo by C.L.D.*

this is evidence enough that Alice's complaint was justified by the punster himself, in whose company both he and others lost their time: and what is more, he is still likely to steal a march on anyone who does not watch out for himself.

The reader may find this conclusion not only somewhat forced, but grotesque. Time was, however, when puns and word-play such as assonance were greeted with respect rather than groans, and were even used by theologians with set purpose.

> āpo'jāyanta arcate vai me kaṁ abhūd iti: tad evārkasya arkatvam: kaṁ ha vā asmai bhavati, ya evam etad arkasya arkatvaṁ veda.

> 'Verily', he thought, 'while I was worshipping [arcate] water appeared, therefore water is called arka [fire]. Water surely comes to one who knows the reason why water is called arka.'
> (*Bṛhad-āraṇyaka Upaniṣad* 1.2.1., translated by Radhakrishnan)

Or, to take an example of alliteration (that is, of head-rhymes) from Arthurian romance:

> The grene knyght upon grounde graythely hym dresses:
> A littel lut with the hede, the lere he discoveres:
> His longe lovelych lokkes he layd over his croun,
> Let the naked nec to the note shewe.
> Gauan gripped to his ax and gederes hit on hyght . . .

> (The Green Knight upon ground girds him with care:
> Bows a little with his head, and bares his flesh:
> His long lovely locks he laid over his crown,
> Let the naked nape for the need be shown.
> Gawain grips to the ax and gathers it aloft . . .)
> (*Sir Gawain and the Green Knight*, translated by Marie Borroff)

The second passage falls neatly to hand, considering what we have said about 'capital' and what we are to say about Anglo-Saxon. But did Carroll know *Gawain*? Perhaps: perhaps not. Perhaps we are dealing with a pun of another kind, namely a coincidence. We shall find plenty of these as we continue, some so odd, neat and crowding thick together that they haunt the imagination. In what spirit are we to take them? Nonsensically, of course: which is to say, with a wry seriousness. For just as puns illuminate the nature of language, so a coincidence sheds light on Nature herself. What we are to make of it is something else, as Carroll can tell us:

> 'Once a coincidence was taking a walk with a little accident, and they met an explanation – a *very* old explanation – so old that it was quite doubled up, and looked more like a conundrum—'
> (*Sylvie and Bruno Concluded*, Chapter XXIII)

The Professor who was telling this story suddenly broke off, because he found it a very difficult sort to invent. We may therefore do the same for the moment, having now intimated to the reader that there is hardly a limit to which Nonsense won't go – and that when it does, it says 'Riddle me, riddle me ree.'

There must *be* a limit, of course, or Nonsense would merely be nonsense. We may find it out by calling to our aid another master of logic, whose Christian name Ludwig bears a happy similarity to that of Charles Dodgson's middle name Lutwidge and who was, like him, a life-long bachelor. Wittgenstein (for it is he) made so bold in his *Tractatus Logico-Philosophicus* as to state that

The *riddle* does not exist.
If a question can be put at all then it *can* also be answered.

We may note in passing that Wittgenstein here is Carrollian in his conversational use of italics, as may be seen by following him up with a passage from *Looking-glass*:

Here the White Queen began again. 'It was *such* a thunderstorm, you ca'n't think!' ('She *never* could, you know,' said the Red Queen.)

This is of interest, for Wittgenstein was such a master of logic that he proved it to be nothing less than tautology: and this in turn, if his way of accenting words is any guide, can be proved to be nothing less than Nonsense. We can therefore assume that Nonsense is a subject for philosophical investigation, and that the Riddle has an answer. But what kind of answer is the problem. Carroll seldom discussed the principles of his own Nonsense – 'Adventures first, explanations take such a dreadful time' being his usual Gryphonesque motto – but Wittgenstein did those of logic. Here then, as a lead-in to Nonsense, is how he begins the Preface to his *Tractatus*:

This book will perhaps only be understood by those who have themselves already thought the thoughts which are expressed in it – or similar thoughts. It is therefore not a text-book. Its object would be attained if it afforded pleasure to one who read it with understanding.

The book deals with the problems of philosophy and shows, as I believe, that the method of formulating these problems rests on the misunderstanding of the logic of our language. Its whole meaning could be summed up as follows: What can be said at all can be said clearly; and whereof one cannot speak thereof one must be silent.

The book will, therefore, draw a limit to thinking, or rather – not to thinking, but to the expression of thoughts; for in order to draw a limit to thinking we should have been able to think both sides of this limit (we should therefore have been able to think what cannot be thought).

The limit can, therefore, only be drawn in language and what lies on the other side of the limit will be simply nonsense.

We might say the same of our own enquiries, but only after we have made a small but revolutionary correction. For when nonsense is given a capital N it allows us to do what Wittgenstein thought impossible, namely, to think on both sides of the limit. It remains true that there are things in Nonsense that cannot be thought, but these do not lie on the *other side* of the limit: they lie *on it*. They are in fact the limit itself, which is therefore not peripheral but central.

All this may appear outlandish. Let me therefore give my own definition of Nonsense. Nonsense, then, is a logical game played with feeling by at least two people, in a spirit of self-contradiction, in such a way that one thing leads on to the other to the constant surprise and mutual enthusiasm of both parties. If there is anything that cannot be spoken of in the game – and there is plenty of that also – it must be looked for at the heart of the self-contradictions that have been put in play by it: and though they are speechless by themselves, they can properly be described as *attitudes*, which comprise some of the things the game leads on to, as well as being those from which it often starts.

Nonsense leads on to so many things that it is not worth our while to particularise them here. For it rests, in Wittgenstein's words, on the misunderstanding of the logic of our language, and it would therefore need a dictionary and grammar even to itemise them. In this it is as all-embracing as Alfred Jarry's 'Pataphysics, defined by its author as 'the science of imaginary solutions, which symbolically attributes the properties of objects, described by their virtuality, to their lineaments'. Roger Shattuck, who quotes this passage in *The Banquet Years* (1959), also says of Jarry that he 'treated ambiguity as the stylistic manifestation of a universal principle of convertibility', which is more immediately to the point. For Nonsense uses the same principle, to such effect that Carroll is a favourite author of those studying nuclear physics, or Time, or mirror-imagery, or logic and semantics, or even Zen Buddhism: their aim being to convert what lies on the other side of the reasonable limit into their particular brand of the Higher Nonsense.

Our enquiry intends to do the same for Carroll and his works, and if the reader can stand the incessant plays on words I must bring to his notice he will eventually find the Nonsense principle of convertibility stated openly, together with its mode of operation and the use Carroll made of it. We can briefly allude to what this last was, via a couplet from *Sylvie and Bruno*:

'Tis a secret: none knows how it comes or it goes:
But the name of the secret is Love!

However, what the secret is *called* is quite another matter, as the White Knight demonstrated in a different context. What, for instance, are we to call *Alice's Adventures in Wonderland*? Is it a fairy-tale, the term Carroll used in his prefatory verses to *Looking-glass*? I think not, if we are to trust Canon Duckworth, who was rowing stroke in the boat that bore Carroll and the three Liddell sisters when the *Adventures* were first told. For he said that it 'was actually composed and spoken *over my shoulder* for the benefit of Alice Liddell, who was acting as "cox" of our gig. I remember turning round and saying, "Dodgson, is this an extempore romance of yours?" And he replied, "Yes, I'm inventing as we go along."' (S. D. Collingwood, *The Lewis Carroll Picture Book*, 1899, p. 358.)

Not a fairy-tale, then, but a romance, in which Alice's hand was being sued for in self-contradictory fashion: because, though the suit was in Hearts, it all ended with a Trial. Moreover, it will appear that Carroll was looking at Alice's cards while telling her the story over Duckworth's shoulder. All this deserves being taken at face

value for, as Walter Besant said, *Alice* is one of the few books that can be read with pleasure by old and young alike: indeed, that 'it is the only child's book of nonsense that is never childish'. The immediate reason for this has been told us by Duckworth, though he rather played down his part in the proceedings: for he seems to have been one of the very few grown-ups, excluding Carroll's relatives, who were ever present while Carroll extemporised a romance to a young girl.

This, then, is the secret we shall be looking into, together with some of the terms that enter into Carroll's principle of convertibility. As we can see, they deal with three different meanings of the word 'court': court cards, courting a minor, and landing up in court. These point plainly enough to why there was a secret, and accounts for that half-intrigued, half-censorious feeling that may bring out the amateur psychoanalyst in us. This priggishness must be resisted, if only to preserve our sense of humour – for why should anyone wish to read Nonsense unless it tickles him? Besides, we are not dealing with a case so much as an art-form, one of the most extraordinary ever developed: it being at once logical, romantic, and extempore.

Those who have tried to deliver an extempore romance to a small audience will know what this entails; and if they come across one that is not only a classic but readable by young and old, they can only salute its author with admiration. True, their admiration may be tempered by a certain disquiet, but this is hardly to the point: it may only mean that they have never flirted with a young girl while flirting with language, logic, mathematics and metaphysics at the same time. We can only stand amazed by Carroll's performance, and his mastery of the extempore mode. Is there any point in trying to *explain* this? Surely not, if we ourselves cannot do half as well.

Let us then put ourselves in Carroll's shoes. 'I distinctly remember, now as I write, how, in a desperate attempt to strike out some new line of fairy-lore, I had sent my heroine straight down a rabbit-hole, to begin with, without the least idea what was to happen afterwards . . .' ('"Alice" on the Stage', 1887.) He said as much to Duckworth, and he also had the Hatter say as much when challenged over the Riddle. In Nonsense, then, one never knows what one is going to say until one has said it. What then prevents one from overstepping the limits set by the meaning of 'court'? Nothing, it seems, but the presence of another grown-up. But which one? The one that may enjoy the story told in his presence to a young girl, or the one the young girl may grow up into? Or both? It must be both, or it wouldn't be Nonsense: and we may thus add that Nonsense consists, in part, of keeping others in their place while putting them through peculiar adventures. However, one cannot do this without an idea of the kind of adventure the other would like to be put through. If, then, there is to be an extempore performance, it must be a joint production, as Gertrude Chataway wrote that it indeed was:

> One thing that made his stories particularly charming to a child was that he often took his cue from her remarks – a question would set him off on a quite new trail of ideas, so that one felt that one had somehow helped to make the story, and it seemed a personal possession.
>
> (S. D. Collingwood, *The Life and Letters of Lewis Carroll*, 1898, p. 380)

Much the same is true for any reader who is sufficiently intrigued by Carroll's charm to lend himself to the Nonsense mode in his turn. He must, of course, do so according to the rules, which he can discover by asking Carroll questions and making him take his cue from the trail of ideas set up in his reader's mind. Carroll will always answer, if not from between the covers of the two *Alices*, then from his other Nonsense works, from his pamphlets dealing with Oxford, from his books on logic and geometry, from his verse, acrostics, puzzles and games, from his diaries and his life and letters. What emerges will be something of a personal possession, though bought at the cost of having one's self turned into an imitation Carroll for the duration: a just price, based on the very *raison d'être* of Nonsense.

With these remarks the reader now has the gist of the argument, and some inkling of the posture he must take up if he wishes to enjoy what follows. Let us therefore set on, first by quoting the chapter that celebrates the Mad Tea-party, for those who have no *Wonderland* to hand; which done, we shall follow Nonsense from one thing to another, and formulate its principles by calling the state of play as we go along.

# A Mad Tea-party

There was a table set out under a tree in front of the house, and the March Hare and the Hatter were having tea at it: a Dormouse was sitting between them, fast asleep, and the other two were using it as a cushion, resting their elbows on it, and talking over its head. 'Very uncomfortable for the Dormouse,' thought Alice; 'only as it's asleep, I suppose it doesn't mind.'

The table was a large one, but the three were all crowded together at one corner of it. 'No room! No room!' they cried out when they saw Alice coming. 'There's *plenty* of room!' said Alice indignantly, and she sat down in a large arm-chair at one end of the table.

'Have some wine,' the March Hare said in an encouraging tone.

Alice looked all round the table, but there was nothing on it but tea. 'I don't see any wine,' she remarked.

'There isn't any,' said the March Hare.

'Then it wasn't very civil of you to offer it,' said Alice angrily.

'It wasn't very civil of you to sit down without being invited,' said the March Hare.

'I didn't know it was *your* table,' said Alice: 'it's laid for a great many more than three.'

'Your hair wants cutting,' said the Hatter. He had been looking at Alice for some time with great curiosity, and this was his first speech.

'You should learn not to make personal remarks,' Alice said with some severity: 'it's very rude.'

The Hatter opened his eyes very wide on hearing this; but all he *said* was 'Why is a raven like a writing-desk?'

'Come, we shall have some fun now!' thought Alice. 'I'm glad they've begun asking riddles – I believe I can guess that,' she added aloud.

'Do you mean that you think you can find out the answer to it?' said the March Hare.

'Exactly so,' said Alice.

'Then you should say what you mean,' the March Hare went on.

'I do,' Alice hastily replied; 'at least – at least I mean what I say – that's the same thing, you know.'

'Not the same thing a bit!' said the Hatter. 'Why, you might just as well say that "I see what I eat" is the same thing as "I eat what I see"!'

'You might just as well say,' added the March Hare, 'that "I like what I get" is the same thing as "I get what I like"!'

'You might just as well say,' added the Dormouse, which seemed to be talking in its sleep, 'that "I breathe when I sleep" is the same thing as "I sleep when I breathe"!'

'It *is* the same thing with you,' said the Hatter, and here the conversation dropped, and the party sat silent for a minute, while Alice thought over all she could remember about ravens and writing-desks, which wasn't much.

The Hatter was the first to break the silence. 'What day of the month is it?' he said, turning to Alice: he had taken his watch out of his pocket, and was looking at it uneasily, shaking it every now and then, and holding it to his ear.

Alice considered a little, and then said 'The fourth.'

'Two days wrong!' sighed the Hatter. 'I told you butter wouldn't suit the works!' he added, looking angrily at the March Hare.

'It was the *best* butter,' the March Hare meekly replied.

'Yes, but some crumbs must have got in as well,' the Hatter grumbled: 'you shouldn't have put it in with the bread-knife.'

The March Hare took the watch and looked at it gloomily: then he dipped it into his cup of tea, and looked at it again: but he could think of nothing better to say than his first remark, 'It was the *best* butter, you know.'

Alice had been looking over his shoulder with some curiosity. 'What a funny watch!' she remarked. 'It tells the day of the month, and doesn't tell what o'clock it is!'

'Why should it?' muttered the Hatter. 'Does *your* watch tell you what year it is?'

'Of course not,' Alice replied very readily: 'but that's because it stays the same year for such a long time together.'

'Which is just the case with *mine*,' said the Hatter.

Alice felt dreadfully puzzled. The Hatter's remark seemed to her to have no sort of meaning in it, and yet it was certainly English. 'I don't quite understand you,' she said, as politely as she could.

'The Dormouse is asleep again,' said the Hatter, and he poured a little hot tea upon its nose.

The Dormouse shook its head impatiently, and said, without opening its eyes. 'Of course, of course: just what I was going to remark myself.'

'Have you guessed the riddle yet?' the Hatter said, turning to Alice again.

'No, I give it up,' Alice replied. 'What's the answer?'

'I haven't the slightest idea,' said the Hatter.

'Nor I,' said the March Hare.

Alice sighed wearily. 'I think you might do something better with the time,' she said, 'than wasting it in asking riddles that have no answers.'

'If you knew Time as well as I do,' said the Hatter, 'you wouldn't talk about wasting *it*. It's *him*.'

'I don't know what you mean,' said Alice.

'Of course you don't!' the Hatter said, tossing his head contemptuously. 'I dare say you never even spoke to Time!'

'Perhaps not,' Alice cautiously replied; 'but I know I have to beat time when I learn music.'

'Ah! That accounts for it,' said the Hatter. 'He wo'n't stand beating. Now, if you only kept on good terms with him, he'd do almost anything you liked with the clock. For instance, suppose it were nine o'clock in the morning, just time to begin lessons: you'd only have to whisper a hint to Time, and round goes the clock in a twinkling! Half-past one, time for dinner!'

('I only wish it was,' the March Hare said to itself in a whisper.)

'That would be grand, certainly,' said Alice thoughtfully; 'but then – I shouldn't be hungry for it, you know.'

'Not at first, perhaps,' said the Hatter: 'but you could keep it to half-past one as long as you liked.'

'Is that the way *you* manage?' Alice asked.

The Hatter shook his head mournfully. 'Not I!' he replied. 'We quarrelled last March—just before *he* went mad, you know—'

(pointing with his teaspoon at the March Hare,) '—it was at the great concert given by the Queen of Hearts, and I had to sing

*"Twinkle, twinkle, little bat!*
*How I wonder what you're at!"*

You know the song, perhaps?'

'I've heard something like it,' said Alice.

'It goes on, you know,' the Hatter continued, 'in this way:

*"Up above the world you fly,*
*Like a tea-tray in the sky.*
*Twinkle, twinkle —* "'

Here the Dormouse shook itself, and began singing in its sleep *'Twinkle, twinkle, twinkle, twinkle—'* and went on so long that they had to pinch it to make it stop.

'Well, I'd hardly finished the first verse,' said the Hatter, 'when the Queen bawled out "He's murdering the time! Off with his head!"'

'How dreadfully savage!' exclaimed Alice.

'And ever since that,' the Hatter went on in a mournful tone, 'he wo'n't do a thing I ask! It's always six o'clock now.'

A bright idea came into Alice's head. 'Is that the reason so many tea-things are put out here?' she asked.

'Yes, that's it,' said the Hatter with a sigh: 'it's always tea-time, and we've no time to wash the things between whiles.'

'Then you keep moving round, I suppose?' said Alice.

17

'Exactly so,' said the Hatter: 'as the things get used up.'

'But what happens when you come to the beginning again?' Alice ventured to ask.

'Suppose we change the subject,' the March Hare interrupted, yawning. 'I'm getting tired of this. I vote the young lady tells us a story.'

'I'm afraid I don't know one,' said Alice, rather alarmed at the proposal.

'Then the Dormouse shall!' they both cried. 'Wake up, Dormouse!' And they pinched it on both sides at once.

The Dormouse slowly opened its eyes. 'I wasn't asleep,' it said in a hoarse, feeble voice, 'I heard every word you fellows were saying.'

'Tell us a story!' said the March Hare.

'Yes, please do!' pleaded Alice.

'And be quick about it,' added the Hatter, 'or you'll be asleep again before it's done.'

'Once upon a time there were three little sisters,' the Dormouse began in a great hurry; 'and their names were Elsie, Lacie, and Tillie; and they lived at the bottom of a well—'

'What did they live on?' said Alice, who always took a great interest in questions of eating and drinking.

'They lived on treacle,' said the Dormouse, after thinking a minute or two.

'They couldn't have done that, you know,' Alice gently remarked. 'They'd have been ill.'

'So they were,' said the Dormouse; '*very* ill.'

Alice tried a little to fancy to herself what such an extraordinary way of living would be like, but it puzzled her too much: so she went on: 'But why did they live at the bottom of a well?'

'Take some more tea,' the March Hare said to Alice, very earnestly.

'I've had nothing yet,' Alice replied in an offended tone: 'so I ca'n't take more.'

'You mean you ca'n't take *less*,' said the Hatter: 'it's very easy to take *more* than nothing.'

'Nobody asked *your* opinion,' said Alice.

'Who's making personal remarks now?' the Hatter asked triumphantly.

Alice did not quite know what to say to this: so she helped herself to some tea and bread-and-butter, and then turned to the Dormouse, and repeated her question. 'Why did they live at the bottom of a well?'

The Dormouse again took a minute or two to think about it, and then said 'It was a treacle-well.'

18    'There's no such thing!' Alice was beginning very angrily, but

the Hatter and the March Hare went 'Sh! Sh!' and the Dormouse sulkily remarked 'If you ca'n't be civil, you'd better finish the story for yourself.'

'No, please go on!' Alice said very humbly. 'I wo'n't interrupt you again. I dare say there may be *one*.'

'One, indeed!' said the Dormouse indignantly. However, he consented to go on. 'And so these three little sisters – they were learning to draw, you know—'

'What did they draw?' said Alice, quite forgetting her promise.

'Treacle,' said the Dormouse, without considering at all, this time.

'I want a clean cup,' interrupted the Hatter: 'let's all move one place on.'

He moved on as he spoke, and the Dormouse followed him: the March Hare moved into the Dormouse's place, and Alice rather unwillingly took the place of the March Hare. The Hatter was the only one who got any advantage from the change; and Alice was a good deal worse off than before, as the March Hare had just upset the milk-jug into his plate.

Alice did not wish to offend the Dormouse again, so she began very cautiously: 'But I don't understand. Where did they draw the treacle from?'

'You can draw water out of a water-well,' said the Hatter; 'so I should think you could draw treacle out of a treacle-well – eh, stupid?'

'But they were *in* the well,' Alice said to the Dormouse, not choosing to notice this last remark.

'Of course they were,' said the Dormouse: 'well in.'

This answer so confused poor Alice, that she let the Dormouse go on for some time without interrupting it.

'They were learning to draw,' the Dormouse went on, yawning and rubbing its eyes, for it was getting very sleepy; 'and they drew all manner of things – everything that begins with an M—'

'Why with an M?' said Alice.

'Why not?' said the March Hare.

Alice was silent.

The Dormouse had closed its eyes by this time, and was going off into a doze; but, on being pinched by the Hatter, it woke up again with a little shriek, and went on: '—that begins with an M, such as mouse-traps, and the moon, and memory, and muchness – you know you say things are "much of a muchness" – did you ever see such a thing as a drawing of a muchness?'

'Really, now you ask me,' said Alice, very much confused, 'I don't think—'

'Then you shouldn't talk,' said the Hatter.

This piece of rudeness was more than Alice could bear: she got up in great disgust, and walked off: the Dormouse fell asleep instantly, and neither of the others took the least notice of her going, though she looked back once or twice, half hoping that they would call after her: the last time she saw them, they were trying to put the Dormouse into the teapot.

'At any rate I'll never go *there* again!' said Alice, as she picked her way through the wood. 'It's the stupidest tea-party I ever was at in all my life!'

Just as she said this, she noticed that one of the trees had a door leading right into it. 'That's very curious!' she thought. 'But everything's curious to-day. I think I may as well go in at once.' And in she went.

Once more she found herself in the long hall, and close to the little glass table. 'Now, I'll manage better this time,' she said to herself, and began by taking the little golden key, and unlocking the door that led into the garden. Then she set to work nibbling at the mushroom (she had kept a piece of it in her pocket) till she was about a foot high: then she walked down the little passage; and *then* – she found herself at last in the beautiful garden, among the bright flower-beds and the cool fountains.

# The stutter,
# relatively speaking

*Alice's Adventures in Wonderland* was first published in 1865, and it caught the public's fancy. It contains so many baited hooks that this is not surprising: and of these, the Riddle was one of the most successful, as Carroll had no doubt intended it to be. But when the 'Eighty-Sixth Thousand of the 6/– edition' was issued in 1896, he thought it was time (as it proved to be, since he died a year later) to make a small confession. It appeared in the Preface:

> Enquiries have been so often addressed to me, as to whether any answer to the Hatter's Riddle can be imagined, that I may as well put on record here what seems to me to be a fairly appropriate answer, viz. 'Because it can produce a few notes, though they are *very* flat; and it is never put with the wrong end in front!' This, however, is merely an afterthought: the Riddle, as originally invented, had no answer at all.

Anyone foolhardy enough to take issue with this bland piece of Nonsense soon finds himself in a circular argument. What kind of note, for instance, is thus put on record, that tries to answer the Riddle with notes said to be false as soon as uttered? Is this a riddle on its own? It is certainly a dark saying, as befits its raven origin, and it is made darker by the second part of the afterthought. For how could anyone *put* a raven with its wrong end in front?

We are left with the suspicion that Carroll was not being entirely trustworthy, if only because a master of the extempore mode must know that a riddle *can* only have an afterthought for an answer. It seems, indeed, to be a put-on, like the Riddle itself. To determine the truth of this, we cannot do better than take a leaf out of another of Carroll's works – the Dodgsonian *Curiosa Mathematica*, Part II: *A New Theory of Parallels* (1888), to be precise. The question is raised there in Appendix II as:

## Is Euclid's Axiom True?

> The answer I propose to give to this alarming proposition is that, though true in the sense *he meant it*, it is *not* true in the sense in which *we take it*.

This gives us enough grounds to conclude that a riddle demanding to be heard but not answered cannot be permitted. Others have felt the same, and have tried to stop its mouth with such telling replies as 'Because they both should be made to shut up.' This comes from the ingenious Sam Loyd, who also proposed 'Because Poe wrote on both', which makes one think; 'Because bills and tales are amongst their characteristics', for which much might be said (and will be); and 'Because the notes for which they are noted are not noted to be musical notes.' (True.) A. Cyril Pearson suggested 'Because it slopes with a flap', which is as it may be; and E. V. Rieu used the ancient back-hander, 'Because "Both" begins with a B.'

This last fails grammatically, and I am indebted to James Michie for his emendation: 'Because "Each" begins with an E.' However, there are good reasons to think that Rieu was essentially correct, and that his solution – together with the others we have quoted – can be proved to be so according to the rules of Nonsense. Indeed, Rieu's solution and Sam Loyd's 'Because they both should be made to shut up' are admirable in taking away with one hand what they give with the other, which is the essence of the game. Here, in honour of the Tea-party at which the Riddle was asked, is a sample from Carroll's *Dynamics of a Parti-cle* (1865), stating the matter plainly. The title-page is embellished, for a start, with the not entirely misleading quotation:

> ''Tis strange the mind, that very fiery particle,
> Should let itself be snuff'd out by an article.'★

and leads on to

---

★The couplet contains one and the Riddle two, both indefinite.

> 'But that's the point!' the young man cried,
>   'The puzzle that I wish to pen you in –
> How are the public to decide
>   *Which* articles are genuine?'
>             ('The Majesty of Justice', 1863)

This is certainly true of the *Dynamics*, where the problem of the 39 Articles is dimly in the offing. Rather than go into this, I give Carroll's definition of 'mind':

> 'Mind – I believe – is Essence – Ent –
> Abstract – that is – an Accident –
> Which we – that is to say – I meant – '
>             ('The Three Voices', 1856)

# GENERAL CONSIDERATIONS
*Definitions*

### I

PLAIN SUPERFICIALITY is the character of a speech, in which any two points being taken, the speaker is found to lie wholly with regard to those two points.

Let us then take it that the Riddle is an example of Plain Superficiality, and see how this definition (carelessly omitting four others about Plain, Right and Obtuse Anger) may be used according to Carroll's own

*Postulates*

### I

Let it be granted, that a speaker may digress from any one point to any other point.

### II

That a finite argument (i.e. one finished and disposed of), may be produced to any extent in subsequent debates.

### III

That a controversy may be raised about any question, and at any distance from that question.

To which we need only add that the arguments we use may often be circular and can, if necessary, be produced to infinity; and that the questions they deal with will be found, on the whole, to lie in parallel.

They will also lie in context. Of course, the context in which the Riddle is asked does not encourage one to expect any of the usual kinds of answer. The hope is present, however, and it seems that the answer is there all along, only waiting for the right moment to be given. But what happens? As soon as Alice enters into the spirit of the thing, she is rebuffed by the Hatter's controversial digression about whether 'I mean what I say' is the same as 'I say what I mean', after which the conversation lapses. The Hatter is the first to break the silence by asking a question – or is it another riddle? – about what day of the month it is. There is then some talk about his watch, and the Dormouse falls asleep again. This is the moment the Hatter chooses to ask Alice whether she has guessed the riddle yet, but is it not too late for that? – two days too late, in a manner of speaking? The thread seems to have been lost, and without it an afterthought – especially one thirty-one years old – is bound to be a bit flat. That is not to say that it is irrelevant: that is, if we add an unimpeachable Postulate of our own:

## IV

*That a statement made while looking backwards will have its wrong end in front.*

One of the finest examples of the workings of this Postulate is to be found in the afterthought prefaced to *The Hunting of the Snark*. It begins:

> *If* – and the thing is wildly possible – the charge of writing nonsense were ever brought against the author of this brief but instructive poem, it would be based, I feel convinced, on the line

'Then the bowsprit got mixed with the rudder sometimes.'

This 'painful possibility' was due, Carroll continued, to the bowsprit being unshipped once or twice a week to be revarnished, and then being fastened on, anyhow, across the stern. During these bewildering intervals the ship usually sailed backwards, the vessel being 'so to speak, "snarked"'.

We do not need the Freudian prosecutor who may be heard muttering 'Bowsprit? once or twice a week? to be varnished?' but the Snark himself, who can manage well enough on his own. Like the dog Fury in the Mouse's Tale, he starts as Counsel for the Defence, and quietly arrogates to himself the duties of Prosecutor, Jury, Witness, and Judge. Ending as a Boojum, his Agony takes Eight Fits. You might call this a circular argument pretending to be an octave.

'But what happens when you come round to the beginning again?' Alice ventured to ask as the Hatter *et al.* kept moving about the Tea-table. That's easy – you change the subject. The same is true if you're doing lessons with the Mock Turtle, starting with ten hours the first day, nine hours the second, and so on. The eleventh day is a holiday, of course. And the twelfth? That's enough about lessons, as the Gryphon said.

We may as well call it Vanishing Day, in honour of the bowsprit. Its victim, of course, was the Baker, who could never change the subject because he did not even know his own name, and whose speciality was Bridecake for which, Carroll was pleased to say, no materials were to be had.★ We shall defer consideration of this path to Boojumry and follow rather the one whose end lies more literally in its beginning with a B.

*The Hunting of the Snark* is full of Bs. We have already noticed the bowsprit: and it is a matter of coincidental interest that, according

---

★ Because, to quote the answer to one of his syllogisms, 'Wedding-cake always disagrees with me.' (*Symbolic Logic*, 1895.)

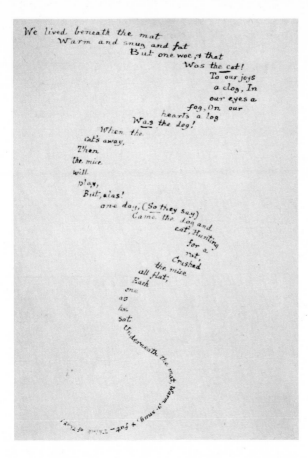

We lived beneath the mat
Warm and snug and fat
But one woe, & that
Was the cat!
To our joys
a clog, In
our eyes a
fog, On our
hearts a log
Was the dog!
When the
cat's away,
Then
the mice
will
play,
But, alas!
one day, (So they say)
Came the dog and
cat, Hunting
for a
rat,
Crushed
the mice
all flat;
Each
one
as
he
sat;
Underneath the mat.

to Webster, 'bees' can refer to 'pieces of wood bolted to the sides of the bowsprit, to reeve the fore-topmast stays through'. Be this as it may, the poem opens with the Bellman landing his crew with care. There are nine of them, all named with a B- after a trade, including a Beaver who certainly must have worked like one to have been included. (The other reasons for his presence will be found in Chapter XII.) It is as well to list them here, since they all have to do with matters germane to the later development of our argument. They are:

Bellman                             Billiard-marker
Boots                               Banker
A maker of Bonnets and Hoods        Beaver
Barrister                           Baker
Broker                              Butcher

25

The poem ends with a Boojum. This provides us with a lesson in eleven steps, and amateurs of coincidence may be pleased to learn that the game of Happy Families into which Carroll was born likewise numbered eleven – excluding the parents – three of them stutterers, and most of the others suffering from minor speech defects.

Having established this parallel, is it disappointing to find that none of Carroll's sisters and brothers had a name beginning with B? Not really: for if we lay out his family tree, we shall find the B at the beginning, ready to pass through four generations disguised as C.★

Right Reverend Charles Dodgson

Captain Charles
Dodgson = Lucy Hume

Elizabeth    Major Charles
Anne Dodgson = Lutwidge

Hassard Dodgson =
Caroline Hume

Reverend              Frances Jane
Charles Dodgson = Lutwidge

Frances Jane
Elizabeth Lucy
Charles Lutwidge
Caroline Hume
Mary Charlotte
Skeffington Hume
Wilfred Longley
Louisa Fletcher
Margaret Anne Ashley
Henrietta Harrington
Edwin Heron

---

★Prove it! prove it! how can that be?
  'Why, what does "B sharp" (in music) mean
  If not "the natural C"?'

('A Sea Dirge', 1861)

I must also put on record here that Carroll's earliest *nom-de-plume* was 'B.B.'. He did not say what he meant by these initials, but his allusion to B♯ points to the fact that B is 'the nominal of the 7th tone of the model major scale' (Webster) and that B♭ is pronounced as by Raven. But he may also have been referring to the first casting of Big Ben at Stockton-on-Tees in 1857. The bell was discovered to have a flaw, and soon after the whole country knew that Big Ben was cracked.

" Oh what bait's that upon your hook
  Dear brother, tell to me ? "
" It is my younger brother," he cried,
  " Oh woe and dole is me !

" I's mighty wicked, that I is !
  Or how could such things be ?
Farewell, farewell sweet sister,
  I'm going o'er the sea."

Just as Frances Jane is named after her mother, and Elizabeth Lucy after her two grandmothers, so Charles Lutwidge is named after his father and his two grandfathers. It was, moreover, a cousinly family – Carroll's parents were first cousins, so were his uncle and aunt, and so the son by Lucy Hume's second marriage and his wife. In addition we find eight Charleses, some of them feminised as Caroline or Charlotte: and we could add another three by taking the Lutwidge line into consideration. This also makes a total of eleven, though later a twelfth was added in the form of Mary Charlotte's husband. (She, Wilfred and Edwin were the only ones of Carroll's siblings to marry.) We may safely conclude from this that Christian names are liable to begin with C – including that of Carroll's great-great-grandfather, who was called Christopher.

Christopher was a vicar. Carroll was a deacon, his father first a canon, and then an archdeacon. And his great-grandfather? B for Bishop – the Bishop of Ossory and Ferns, later translated to the See of Elphin.

This, so far, is but a curiosity, as is the fact that after Carroll discarded the title of 'Alice's Adventures Underground', and before he took Dean Liddell's suggestion to call the book *Alice's Adventures in Wonderland*, he was toying with the idea of calling it 'Alice's Adventures in Elfland'. Yet, where are the elves in *Wonderland*? And where, to be equally severe with ourselves, is the Bishop?

That is easy enough – in *Looking-glass*, much of which had already been told to Alice before *Wonderland* was written, especially those episodes that deal with chessmen. Four Bishops are to be found there, though not mentioned by *name* – you can only find who they are by consulting the Dramatis Personae thoughtfully provided to show how the plot is based on a chess game. The two Red Bishops turn out to be the Walrus and the Crow; the White ones, the Sheep and the Aged Aged Man of the White Knight's Wordsworthian parody.

This is an odd set. The Carpenter is not a Bishop like his companion the Walrus, but a Knight; but this is no accident, for Carroll suggested two other names for the character, the Baronet and the Butterfly, leaving Tenniel to make the final choice. The Sheep is what happened when the White Queen cried, 'Oh, much better! ... Much be-etter! Be-etter! Be-e-e-etter! Be-e-ehh!' so that she at least starts off like a Bishop. The Crow cannot be a Rook, and should not be mistaken for a raven by any competent ornithologist, though a Nonsense master will have other ideas, especially if his mother was born in the village of Holmrook close to the town of Ravenglass. (For more on this, see Chapter XII.) As for the Aged Aged Man, he is not only the caricature of Wordsworth's Leech Gatherer, the incarnation of Resolution and Independence, but Carroll himself, for he dubbed himself by that phrase in the whimsical journal he wrote for Isa Bowman after she had visited him in Oxford. (Certainly 'Venerable' is not the proper style by which to address a bishop, such as his grandfather, nor a deacon, Carroll himself: but it is proper for his father the Archdeacon.)

Let us suppose now – and the thing is possible – that Carroll might once have wished to know what it meant to be called Charles Lutwidge Dodgson. He would, by the use of precedents, have found himself regressing down the rabbit-hole of his family and ending as a Bishop. This would be a Nonsensical transformation, giving the first words spoken in *Wonderland* a poignant and apposite significance – 'Oh dear! Oh dear! I shall be too late!' These were, of course, uttered by the White Rabbit, of the kind that is often pulled

out of conjurors' hats. Carroll's hypothetical change into a Bishop might also be justified by one of the seldom-used rules of chess that allows a pawn to be turned into *any* piece when it has reached the other end of the board. This is a great deal more respectable than the 'castling' of the three Queens at the end of *Looking-glass*, which is 'merely a way of saying that they had entered the palace'. However, this justification allows us to point out that a Bishop, being a prince of the Church, also inhabits a palace, and that Carroll's diaries record several occasions when he dined at the palace of the Bishop of Ripon.

This digression has served to introduce the Bishop, who will appear again later, and to give some substance to the fancy that the ch- ch- ch- ch- of Charles Lutwidge Dodgson is in parallel with the b- b- b- b- of the Bellman and his crew. Now these series may

*Members of the Dodgson family at Croft. Photo by C.L.D.*

have something to do with stuttering, but what have they to do with the Riddle? The answer is, m- m- more* than one thinks. To see this clearly, we may start in the middle of the Tea-party, when the Dormouse is telling a story about three little girls called Elsie, Tillie and Lacie, who stand for the three Liddell daughters Carroll was entertaining in his Wonderland. They lived, said the Dormouse, in a treacle-well, and liked drawing – treacle, for a start, and then all manner of things that begin with an M, such as mouse-traps, and the moon, and memory, and muchness. (Alice had some difficulty with this one, though she must often have seen him drawing tea; like Isa Bowman, who wrote: 'He was very particular about his tea, which he always made himself, and in order that it should draw properly he would walk about the room swinging the tea-pot from side to side for exactly ten minutes.' (*The Story of Lewis Carroll*, 1899, p. 36.))

ch- ch- ch- ch-
b- b- b- b-
m- m- m- m- . . .

What precedes? The March Hare has spilt the Milk-jug on his plate, and has criticised Alice for not saying what she Means: the Hatter has asked what day of the Month it is, and confessed to once having Murdered Time. He has done this so effectively that Time not only begins but ends with Tea for him; and he, like the March Hare, is Mad. But why is he never *called* the Mad Hatter? Can it be that, though his name contains all the letters of Hare, his madness has been somewhat watered down in swallowing the initials of Tea-Time?** In any case, the mention of Time sets him off on Twinkling, Tea-Trays, Taking More, and the Dormouse on Treacle.

m- m- m- m-
t- t- t- t-

---

* '"Yes, m'm, Master *is* at home, m'm," said the stately old butler. (N.B. – It is only a butler of experience who can manage a series of three M's together, without any interjacent vowels.)' (*A Tangled Tale*, 1885.)

**This is not an impossibility, for Carroll much enjoyed anagrams and brilliantly converted W. E. Gladstone into 'Wild agitator! Means well'. But the 'Hatter: Hare-T.T.' transformation is obviously on a different level, which can be paralleled elsewhere – for instance, in the fact that Layard, who is cited in the Tailpiece, called his book *The Lady of the Hare*. Anagrammatising this we find that 'Layard' goes into 'Lady' and 'Hare' leaving him as his own subject.

Since we have started at the middle, let us now push back one whole chapter to the time when the Cheshire Cat says that everyone in the story must be mad to be there at all, itself included. For, it said, granted that a dog is not mad to growl when angry (but let us use the right word – in a Fury) and wag its tail when pleased, the Cat growls when pleased and wags its tail when angry. Therefore . . .

gr- gr- gr- gr-

Growls? Alice calls it purring, but the Cat just Grins, which may be the right word for that. It grins on and on, even when it has vanished. What does that remind one of?

> In the midst of the word he was trying to say,
> In the midst of his laughter and glee,
> He had softly and suddenly vanished away –
> For the Snark *was* a Boojum, you see.

We must conclude from this that a B can indeed pass disguised as a C (and a great many other letters, such as S for Snark) if the Cheshire Cat's disappearing act is anything like that of the Boojum. The technique should come easily to a stutterer: we may imagine the Baker crying out 'It's a Snark!' without hesitation, but getting fatally entrapped in the horror of pronouncing b-b-b-b-Boojum. What is more, as A. L. Taylor has remarked in *The White Knight* (1952, p. 178), Carroll learnt to take full advantage of his impediment when telling a story, by using the verbal crisis to prolong the dramatic one. He must also have mastered another trick, that of abandoning a word that jammed his mouth for a synonym that came more easily. By 1875, the year he finished composing the *Snark*, he realised the inexpressible pitch to which this art could be developed, as an entry in his diary tells us.

Dec. 31. I declined my usual role of story-teller in the morning, and so (I hope) broke the rule of always being expected to.

Hence the Boojum of silence that swallowed speaker and speech at the end of the *Snark*. But here we must pause. Can it be at the end, when a ship is snarked by having its bowsprit mixed up with its rudder? It is in fact at the beginning in the most literal fashion, for the last line of the *Snark* was the first to come to Carroll when he was having a walk near Guildford in 1874, and the rest of the poem followed. It should therefore be read on a writing-desk which is put with its wrong end in front, as the one which is like a raven is said not to be.

31

We shall discover just what a Boojum is in due course. Meanwhile we have the Cheshire Cat to examine, whose disappearing trick was seemingly confined to itself. Its C is a disguise for another B, if only because Cheshire was the County in which Carroll was Born. (I should say, Dodgson, for Carroll only came into existence at Oxford in 1856.) But besides this we must not forget that the Cat had more than a passing interest in the Duchess's Baby.* This also disappeared, leaving a pig in its place.

'Did you say "pig", or "fig"?' the Cat asked, as though it cared one way or the other. Alice replied, 'I said "pig"', adding 'I wish you wouldn't keep appearing and vanishing so suddenly: you make me quite giddy!' And giddy she must have been, since the Cat was then putting the last touches to an elvish mystery that has long plagued mankind, and that is also one of the principal operations of Nonsense. Since a mystery concerns something that cannot openly be spoken of, we must let it unfold itself as we continue: here we shall but note its alliterative course.

For *something* has been appearing and vanishing from the beginning of the chapter. First there is the Fish Footman, delivering a letter to the Frog Footman – a letter from the Queen to the Duchess, inviting her to play croquet. Alice then opens the door of the house, and inside discovers the Duchess, with cook, Cat and baby. There is a cauldron of soup on the boil, with a great deal too much pepper in it; and plates, fire-irons, saucepans and dishes whizz through the

---

*Carroll's nurse, who received the first letter we have record of from him, was called 'Bun'. The facile and unworthy suspicion has sometimes crossed my mind that his first pen-name, 'B.B.', stands for 'Bun's Baby', partly on account of a poem he wrote to Maggie Bowman in 1889:

> They met a Bishop on their way . . .
>   A Bishop large as life,
> With loving smile that seemed to say
>   'Will Maggie by my wife?'
>
> Maggie thought *not*, because, you see,
>   She was so *very* young,
> And he was old as old could be . . .
>   So Maggie held her tongue.
>
> 'My Lord, she's Bootles' Baby, we
>   Are going up and down,'
> Her friend explained . . .

*Bootles' Baby* was a farce first performed in 1856, in which Maggie later played the lead.

air between sneezes. 'Oh, *please* mind what you're doing!' cries Alice. 'Oh, there goes his *precious* nose!' Indeed, a few minutes later the baby gets a snout and starts grunting.

Some letters come alphabetically, such as

A for Alice
B for baby
C for cook, Cat, cauldron
D for Duchess and door

but Carroll did not deliver them in this order. They come, instead, as an interweaving of

f-f-f-f-
p-p-p-p-
c-cr-qu-
sn-
gr-

after which we have

m-m-
gr-gr-gr-gr-
m-m-m-m-
t-t-t-t-

And so on. By this phrase we take for granted that the series will not only continue, but keep the story on its tracks and lead it to a harmonious conclusion. How right we are in this we must leave to the next chapter, for the Riddle is right ahead: and since this also declines its usual role by breaking the rule of having an answer, we need to describe what game is being played in more detail.

# Chapter II

# Rules for retort

The reader should now be aware that anyone looking for Nonsense is in for it, and that to follow its tracks is enough to make the head spin. However, he may gain comfort from the assurance that Nonsense can stop one from being giddy if, continuing to spin, one reverses direction: a practice advocated in another section of the *Dynamics*, namely

PROP. IV. TH.

The end (i.e. 'the product of the extremes'), justifies (i.e. 'is equal to' – see Latin 'aequus'), the means.

We shall do our level best to follow Carroll's example: and to do so we must demonstrate that Nonsense takes the form of a game, and has a set of rules.* This game we may christen 'Anglo-Saxon Attitudes', whose rules will become clear as we comment on the course of play and let our heads spin.

Just what do we mean by 'spin'? Let us equate it now with alliteration, and the antics of a verbal series. We need only look at the personage who incarnates the Attitudes to see the point of this. For he is Haigha, which is Anglo-Saxon for Hare: and if, as we are told, he is loved with an H because he is Happy, that is because it is only when he alliterates that he attitudinises. He is also hated because he is Hideous; he eats Ham-sandwiches and Hay, and lives on the Hill. He is the White King's Messenger, and makes his way slowly because he is the Queen's Knight's Pawn and can only move from one alliteration to another. (The other Messenger is called Hatta, for the King has two, one to come, and one to go.)

The Attitude is thus best seen in March, when Puss (as the hare is often called) goes mad with sexual excitement: and this excitement, where *Wonderland* is concerned, goes on to the dog days, that is, the month of July when the story was first told and rabies are a

---

*This is only another way of stating a proposition in Carroll's *Symbolic Logic*: 'Every idea of mine, that cannot be expressed as a Syllogism, is really ridiculous.' The happy result of following this rule can be found in the answer to the sorites that follows: 'All my dreams come true.'

# The Dog-days.

*The Dog-days.*
*'REMEMBER! there is no cure for the*
*bite of a mad dog.'*
*(Hone's Every Day Book for July 3.)*

" The Dog-star rages."

possibility. As for the principal form of the Attitude, this is demonstrated by the Messenger coming to the point after having gone as far as possible: too much out of breath to say a word, he waves his hands about, rolls his eyes wildly from side to side, and makes the most fearful faces. ("'You alarm me," said the King. "I feel faint – "'")

What rules shall we invent to account for this? The first, plainly, is

Rule 1. *You can come and go simultaneously, as long as there are two of you.*

The others can be developed from what lessons have taught us:

Rule 2. *If you meet yourself when you have gone too far, you are said to disappear.*
Rule 3. *The point from which a circular argument starts is central to it.*
Rule 4. *To change the subject, draw a parallel.*

To these we can add a more general rule:

Rule 5. *Players are obliged to create an appearance, but they score only if it deceives.*

The other rules must wait, because Haigha not only moves slowly but, like Hatta, is mad – which allows us to continue with our series of m- m- m- m-. This series really begins, not with the Cheshire Cat, but its owner, the Duchess: for she was originally both the 35

Queen of Hearts and the Marchioness of Mock Turtle. When 'Alice's Adventures Underground' became *Alice's Adventures in Wonderland* this character, who was addicted to ordering people's heads cut off, turned against itself and, as Rule 1 demands, became two people. The Marchioness (the name was then slang for a slatternly general maid, but she properly should be addressed as 'Madam' and referred to as 'Your Ladyship', a formality caricatured by the White Knight when he was telling Alice the name of his song) then became the Duchess, perhaps because her first title was too obviously echoed by the name of the March Hare.

It is all the same the Cat who, having proved by growling that it is not angry when pleased, leaves the grin on the face of its Madness to continue into the next chapter without visible means of support. It fades away for a time when the DorMouse (who shares a D with the Duchess) has its head stuffed into the Tea-pot. This brings the M and T series into coincidence, and leaves Alice free to find a Door out of the situation, through a Tree and into the next chapter and the Croquet Game. (It's been a game of croquet★ all along, with

one sound hitting another through the hoops.) The grin comes back with the Duchess finding Morals in everything, and then there is the Mock Turtle, who learnt his lessons from an old turtle called Tortoise.

---

★And a game of stuttering, too, if the Tutor in *The Vision of the Three T's* (1873) is to be trusted: 'But indeed a single arch, where folk might smoothly enter in, were wholly adverse to Nature, who formeth never a mouth without setting a tongue as obstacle in the midst thereof.'

'But let us return to our muttons (as our noble allies do most unromantically express themselves)' ('Novelty and Romancement', 1856). Before saying goodbye to the nearly-vanished Cheshire Cat, Alice receives directions on how to find its mad neighbours who, in spite of living in different places, act on similar premises. She then spies the very large house of the March Hare, and decides she is not large enough to confront its inhabitant unless she nibbles at the left-hand piece of Mushroom she has prudently kept in her pocket for just such an emergency. Though the mushroom makes her Grow, she is still timid enough to wonder whether, though it be May, the March Hare may not still be Raving Mad.

m- m- m-
gr- gr- gr-
v-
r- v- m-

The cunning alliteration of these sounds has set the story spinning in one direction, but to preserve its equanimity the spin must now be reversed. Carroll does so by means of the Riddle, the principal lesson of the Mad Tea-party. For we learn that the March Hare is not mad, as Alice had feared, but just not very civil: it and the Hatter, indeed, have no manners. 'No room! No room!' they cry out when she approaches. 'Have some wine,' the March Hare then says, when she has sat down, though there is none. The Hatter makes a personal remark, and Alice reproves him for being rude.

The Hatter opened his eyes very wide on hearing this; but all he *said* was, 'Why is a raven like a writing-desk?'

He must have said this with a growl, for Alice is encouraged to think they can all have fun now they are asking riddles. She believes she can guess that, she says.

What is the question? For the Hatter immediately questioned her understanding of what the March Hare then said, so that there are at least two to be answered:

a) 'Why is a raven like a writing-desk?'
b) Does 'I say what I mean' mean the same as 'I mean what I say'?

which lead on to three others,

c) 'What day of the month is it?'
d) If it's always six o'clock, 'Is that the reason so many tea-things are put out here?'

37

e)  and that being so, 'What happens when you come to the beginning again?'

the series originating in two unspoken ones,

f)  Is it as rude to sit down uninvited as to make personal remarks?
g)  Why did the Hatter's eyes open very wide?

The rules we have so far deduced give us an immediate answer to e), but we shall not take this way out. Let us instead begin in Carrollian fashion, at the end, by answering g), 'Why did the Hatter's eyes open very wide?' The answer is to be found in quite a different rule-book, and was inscribed by Carroll in the copy of *Wonderland* he gave to the daughter of E. A. Litton: 'Little girls should be seen and not heard.' The Tea-party at which Alice gave offence was, however, a Mad one, where the rule governing rudeness goes:

> 'One fixed exception there must be,
> That is, the Present Company.'
>                 ('The Three Voices', 1856)

We may, however, excuse Alice for her lapse for, as she said in *Looking-glass*, 'Manners are not taught in lessons.' This noted, the answer to g) can be stated as

Rule 6.  *Answering back is allowed, as long as you know what is in question.*

Using this, we can move back to f), 'Is it as rude to sit down uninvited as to make personal remarks?' This can be answered, 'If one, then the other; but if not, neither.' The same answer can be given for b), 'Does "I say what I mean" mean the same as "I mean what I say"?' That is, is the Riddle a riddle? To answer this, we must deal with e), 'What happens when you come round to the beginning again?' We know that the fairly appropriate answer to that has to do with things liable to have their wrong end put in front, one of them being the Riddle. That there is another answer goes without saying: but since it has to do with lessons, we shall refrain from giving it until we have reached the vanishing point. Jumping over d) and c), which we shall leave for the moment, we have thus arrived back at a).

Why, then, is a raven like a writing-desk? Because 'Both' begins with a B? No: that, according to Rule 5, scores nothing. A raven is like a writing-desk because it *doesn't* begin with the same letter.

38

You can see the difference – in black and white★ – when you read what Carroll wrote, but you cannot hear it when he's raving. This is only right, since the presence of a mute letter on the desk warns us that we are being taught a lesson about what is not allowed. It is in such plays on words that the sense of the Riddle lies, and so far Carroll was correct in saying that, as invented, it had no answer. How could it have, when it was meant to be an unanswerable retort to Alice's rudeness? It is a piece of Plain Superficiality at its best – so ingenious a conjuring trick, indeed (as was the Hatter's remark that he had not the slightest idea of its answer), that Alice lost its import.★★ The Tea-party was therefore brought to an end by a more brutal exercise in the same genre:

> 'Really, now you ask me,' said Alice, very much confused, 'I don't think—'
> 'Then you shouldn't talk,' said the Hatter.

This syllogistic insult proved too much for Alice, who retreated in disgust; but it allows us to set down

Rule 7.  *As long as you keep your temper, you do not lose the game even by drinking out of someone else's teacup.*

'Retort' is a word that comes from Latin *retorquere*, to twist back: so we have arrived at the moment when the spin of Nonsense changes direction. It will do so several times before we come to Rule 42, that transforms the slight within a retort into an elixir by altering the opening of Rule 7 to read 'As long as you keep another's temper . . .' But the retort itself still claims our attention. For a start, we

---

★ A simple answer to the Riddle thus is, Because it is not red. This goes with our view that Nonsense is a game, a game played in *Wonderland* with red and black cards, and in *Looking-glass* with red and white chessmen. Why not black and white ones? We shall content ourselves here by noting three other games that Carroll enjoyed playing: croquet, played with balls of as many colours as there are players; billiards, with white and red balls; and draughts, with black and white pieces. It is this last game that can answer the Riddle, via the pun made by the Dormouse on 'drawing'.

★★ A double import – the Riddle was teaching her a lesson, and she was having to pay for it. We can thus aptly quote here from Carroll's diatribe against schoolmasters, 'The Palace of Humbug' (1855):

> All birds of evil omen there
> Flood with rich Notes the tainted air,
> The witless wanderer to snare.
>
> The fatal Notes neglected fall . . .

"Be rather in the trumpet's mouth." F Tennyson.

may doubt that Carroll 'invented' it in any but the original sense of the word, namely, by coming upon it* while being spurred on by the needs of the plot on the one hand, and the alliterations he was playing with on the other – by what we may be allowed to call his writing habit. We should, therefore, be able to see how the spin is reversed by examining the alliterative series that led up to and into the party.

m- m- m- m-
gr- gr- gr-
v-n
r-v
m-d

This is enough to go on with if we add that the first words spoken at the party were 'No room!' and then 'Have some wine!' The r-s, v-s and w-s can then be seen to dance a phonetic quadrille, with nasals and dentals changing partners under the influence of the vowel sound 'i' and the patronage of the White Rabbit, thus:

| Rabbit | White |
| raving mad | vanish |
| no room | wine |
| remarks (there are five in four pages) | |
| very rude | eyes wide |
| | why is |
| raven | writing-desk |
| riddles | |

---

*'. . . but whenever or however it comes, *it comes of itself.*' ('"Alice" on the Stage', 1887.)

after which the Hatter takes out his Watch and discovers that it is Wrong.

This double series should convince anyone that the Riddle was indeed an extempore invention, even when we take *extempore* in its etymological sense of 'out of time'. Here Rule 3 comes into force, since a circular argument immediately follows whose central point obeys Euclidean logic in being without dimension, and Carrollian method in being a piece of Plain Superficiality; while the argument it produces follows Rule 5, in consisting of deceptive appearances.

I call it an argument for form's sake, though it might just as well be called a fourfold answer to the Riddle. It begins with Alice attempting an answer and being immediately rebuffed by the March Hare, following the Hatter, who asks whether 'I mean what I say' is the same as 'I say what I mean'.★

We may take it that the first phrase refers to the raven, and the second to the writing-desk. The three other statements and their inversions then effectively bring the extempore movement to a stop. For the Hatter continues his lesson in table-manners by objecting, 'You might just as well say that "I see what I eat" is the same thing as "I eat what I see"!' The King of Hearts had the same habit of tabling objections which he then read out from his notebook as rules: and as the Trial scene has to do with Who Stole The Tarts, we shall permit ourselves to extend the meaning of *raven* into *ravenous*, which the Hatter must have been if tea was his only meal. Having done so, the meaning of 'I eat what I see' must be looked for on the writing-desk, where it might well appear as the old adage that to study is to read, mark, learn and inwardly digest.

The Hare follows: 'You might just as well say that "I like what I get" is the same thing as "I get what I like"!' Since 'like' is the operative word in the Riddle, this tells us that the Hare gets the raven and the writing-desk whatever he likes – that is, the same kind of used goods that come to him when the Hatter decides to move on one place, and the Hare finds himself where the Dormouse was. But he can hardly object to this, because the Dormouse's contribution is to say that 'I breathe when I sleep' is the same as 'I sleep when I breathe': and since this entails no contradiction, we can take it that his plate is always clean. It is at this moment that the conversation drops, with the dancers of the alliterative quadrille having completed the first figure.

Hidden in all these goings-on is another riddle, the one that ends *Looking-glass* with the chapter entitled 'Which dreamed it?' As Alice says then, 'You see, Kitty, it *must* have been either me or the Red

---

★As for what 'mean' might mean in this context, see page 49.

41

King. He was part of my dream, of course – but then I was part of his dream too!' And both, of course, were part of Carroll's daydream since he was wide awake when telling the stories of *Wonderland* and *Looking-glass*. But does any of this refer to the Riddle itself? Yes: because, on the one hand, the chapter in which Alice *meets* the Red King ends with the advent of the Monstrous Crow; and on the other, because if we subtract 'Red King' from 'writing-desk', the remainder will quite take away one's wits: it's w.

We shall see later that the doubling of a proposition on itself creates a product that must likewise be inverted before a definitive piece of Nonsense is achieved. As a conversation stopper, the Riddle does not pass through this process openly, though the fourfold argument tells us that it is doing so under cover. However, the allusions that it gives rise to are so numerous and diffuse that the operation can hardly be performed with exactitude. Nor can a single answer properly do justice to it, unless we count the Riddle as its own answer – which we might well do, since it speaks for itself.

But there is more, as Lévi-Strauss would say. There must be, of course, for though we have put raven and writing in parallel with raving and reading, we have left out the desk. It was on this desk that Carroll wrote out the story he had told Alice during the boating party, some months after the event. The Tea-party with its disingenuous rudeness was not in the first version, but was added when Carroll decided to rewrite it for publication. R. L. Green in his edition of the *Alices* (1971) has suggested that it was first told at Alice's birthday party on May 4, the date being given by Alice during the Tea-party and in the previous chapter. Even so, it was certainly written up afterwards, as the precision of the argument bears witness.

But the desk? This was not one at which you sit, but at which you stand.* And if you use it for reading and not for writing, what then? It becomes a lectern. On it, supported by the wings of an unanswerable raven, lies – not the Scriptures, not a sermon, not just a riddle, but the Riddle itself, fresh from the same inkpot that the enraged Queen of Hearts was later to throw at the jury during the Trial scene. A notable place for an ink-slinger, in fact, on which an objector like Carroll had no difficulty in tabling his 'No'.

Plain Superficiality demands that we look, if only in a digression, at the truth that lies on a lectern. Since we have already changed the bird supporting it from an eagle to a raven, we can change it

---

\* 'Now that's a thing *I will not stand*,
And so I tell you flat.'
('Phantasmagoria', Canto III)

once more into a crow; and that, of course, is a Bishop. Here then is the Right Reverend Charles, Bishop of Ossory, preaching a sermon in the church of St Canice, on the text: 'My Son, fear thou the Lord, and the King' (Proverbs xxiv. 21); the text being published at the request of

> The JUDGES of Assize, for the LEINSTER Circuit;
> The MAYOR and CITIZENS of KILKENNY:
> The HIGH SHERIFF,
> AND
> The GENTLEMEN of the GRAND JURY.

In this sermon, the Bishop lays down the Law in its most awful and traditional form. He examines the nature of Judgment, Obedience and Right Witness, about which he says:

Can any vice be more pernicious than that, which misrepresents the nature of things, and substitutes delusions for realities with a design to mislead the judgment in its most important determination?

after which he comes to the thunderous conclusion:

As to you, whose duty it is *to bind and to loose* according to the state of the case under examination . . . Consider that you yourselves must stand in the last day before the judgment-seat of God. Upon the sentence, which you now pass on others, in part depends that most awful and irreversible one, which will then be passed on you.

Our first witness is a dean, the father of Carroll's heroine:

I have heard that boys used to say they could not tell Liddell a lie and look him in the face; and I have heard him say 'I can call no man a gentleman if he can act a lie, even if he does not tell it.'

(F. Markham, *Recollections of a Town Boy at Westminster*, 1903)

And the second witness is a deacon, who preached little because he stuttered much:

I have not yet been able to get the 2nd vol: Macaulay's *England* to read: I have seen it however & one passage struck me when 7 bishops signed the invitation to the pretender, & King James sent for Bishop Compton (who was one of the 7) & asked him 'whether he or any of his ecclesiastical brethren had had anything to do with it?' He replied after a moment's thought, 'I am fully persuaded, your majesty, that there is not one of my brethren who is not as innocent as myself.' This was certainly no actual

43

lie, but certainly, as Macaulay says, it was very little different from one. On the next day the king called a meeting of all the bishops, when Compton was present, but the other 6 absented themselves. He then for form's sake put the question to each of them 'whether they had had anything to do with it?' Here was a new difficulty, which Compton got over by saying, when it came to his turn, 'I gave your lordship *my* answer yesterday.' It certainly showed talent, though exerted in the wrong direction . . .

(Letter to his sister Elizabeth, May 4, 1849)

To discover the Defendant in this case, it is enough to make him stand in that kind of pulpit which has no lectern, i.e. the Dock. He then turns out to be the Hatter. It is true that in *Wonderland* he is merely in the Witness Stand, but in *Looking-glass* he has just come

out of prison, so he must have been found guilty of something. As his offence is not mentioned there, we must turn back to *Wonderland* to find that he was originally charged with murdering the time.

The offence was committed at the Concert of the Queen of Hearts,★ when he was singing. The Concert must have been held at six o'clock in the afternoon, for otherwise it would not always be tea-time with the Hatter, and two days wrong at that. In this situation he was also found guilty of wasting time by asking a riddle whose answer, he

---

★ 'March 8, 1856. Went to the Deanery in the evening to a musical party. I took the opportunity of making friends with little Lorina Liddell, the second of the family.'

said, he had no idea of. After all we have said on this topic, can we yet find the Hatter guilty of telling a lie? For if a master of Nonsense intends to put a girl in her place by extemporising a riddle, it follows that he comes to the answer when she is there. Taking our cue from that other master, Sam Loyd, we can read the intention directly into the answer, which then must be 'Shut up'.

It is difficult to make the charge of lying stick, because the Hatter indeed made Alice shut up by wasting her time with a digression (as she must have thought): and this being so, to give a plain answer when challenged would have been both vulgar and tautological. But we can bring another charge, brought up by the Queen's cry of 'Off with his head!' whose substance can be put as

Rule 8. *The Player who cannot answer the question he has asked himself will be executed. This entails an indefinite loss of time in prison, until the trial comes to a head again.*

This later trial occurs in *Looking-glass* when the Lion and the Unicorn are fighting for the Crown: and since Hatta is there as witness, fresh from prison, we must find the second charge proved. But we have not finished with it or Rule 8 which, as may be gathered from the Bishop's sermon, is the one that will be held against you on the last day. It dates from at least the 7th or 8th century BC, when the *Bṛhad-āraṇyaka Upaniṣad* was written, with the following story of Sakalya. This Brahmin set himself up to examine Yajnavalkya, who was not so much a Brahmin as the relentlessly explanatory voice of Brahma Himself.

'How many gods are there, Yajnavalkya?' asked Sakalya.

Yajnavalkya, who naturally knew his own scriptures by heart, answered: 'As many as are mentioned in the invocation of the hymn of praise to the Visve-devas, namely, three thousand and three, and three hundred and three.'

'Yes, but how many gods are there, Yajnavalkya?' asked Sakalya.

Yajnavalkya, his foot set on what was the original Eight-fold Way, answered thirty-three; and then, six; and then three, two, one and a half, and one. He knew the nature of all these gods, and their names, and their supports: the whole hierarchy, down to its source in the human heart.

'Yes, but on what is the heart supported?' asked Sakalya.

It might be thought that Yajnavalkya, by applying Rule 1, could have answered: 'On three thousand and three, and on three hundred and three.' But this was impossible, because he knew the Self he talked of in such a way that he and it were no longer two. He could also have appealed to Rule 9, which I will state in a moment. But what he said was: 'If you do not explain that to me your head will fall off.' Sakalya did not know the answer, and his head fell off. 'Indeed, robbers took away his bones, thinking they were something else' – a critique of Nonsense, perhaps.

Rule 9.  *The description of a circle does not explain the point it is drawn from.*

This goes counter to our assertion that the description of an intent gives the answer to a riddle: but we were talking of a Riddle, and have said nothing about a Circle. (We have, of course, alluded to it in its diminutive form, a circlet or crown: but we shall leave this till Chapter IX.) But since we have in some measure described a circle, we shall mark the fact by drawing to a stop, and reserve to the next chapter the discussion of its point.

Chapter III

# The double-you

The theory involved in the foregoing Proposition is at present much controverted, and its supporters are called upon to show what is the fixed *point*, or *locus standi*, on which they propose to effect the necessary revolution.

*(The Dynamics of a Parti-cle)*

We here have justification for Rule 9 which is, of course, a development of Rule 3: and with its aid we can rephrase the Riddle thus (for the final answer has by no means been given to it):

When a circular argument is snarked, on what is it supported?

On the bowsprit? the rudder? the ship?
On the sea?
On the Boojum?

Dare we, with the Bakerish fate of Sakalya in mind, ask about the Boojum? That will depend on the language we use. For instance (even if you are not a stutterer), you must have noticed 'the curious phenomenon . . . that if you repeat a word a great many times in succession, however suggestive it may have been when you began, you will end by divesting it of every shred of meaning, and almost wondering how you could ever have meant anything by it!' ('The Stage and the Spirit of Reverence', 1888.)

Or you may be a geometrician, attempting to disprove that the impossible cannot happen. '"What sane man would expect, on finding an equilateral triangular board, which would exactly fit *inside* the mouth of a well, to be able to lay that same board safely down, with its three corners resting *on the edges* of the well? Surely the thing is absurd!" And it almost looked as though I had caught the Will o' the Wisp at last!' (*A New Theory of Parallels.*)

Or you could be a philosopher: 'Now it is not possible – this, I think, all psychologists will admit – by an effort of volition, to carry out the resolution "I will *not* think of so and so."' (*Curiosa Mathematica*, Part II.)

Or you could be the mother overheard by Carroll calling her young son Boojum. He was delighted by someone else knowing the name well enough to know what it stood for! But wasn't it common knowledge?

Baby, baby, naughty baby,
Hush, you squalling thing, I say,
Peace this moment, peace, or maybe
Bonaparte will pass this way . . .

And he'll beat you, beat you, beat you,
And he'll beat you all to pap,
And he'll eat you, eat you, eat you,
Every morsel, snap, snap, snap.

(I. and P. Opie, *Oxford Dictionary of Nursery Rhymes*, 1951)

Babies enjoy the idea of being eaten in this way: it's back down the rabbit-hole for them and into the garden, where there's no need to go Boohoo. When they are older, of course, the ploy requires more severity, as in the one Carroll used on his brother, aged 6:

Dear Skeff,
    Roar not, lest thou be abolished.

Having thus asked about the Boojum, we find the answer composes itself into something it is impossible not to think of by an effort of will, though it can be held at bay by telling stories (in which it will appear as a joke), or by thinking about something else – the Pillow Problems Carroll set himself to solve at night to keep 'unholy thoughts' away, for instance, or ambitious attempts to catch the Will-o'-the-wisp. It could be made to disappear by the use of repetition or regression, except that the disappearance of meaning which this entails is itself a mark of the Boojum. It thus appears to be something of a non-entity, whose nature we need to particularise further, if we can; for we still have the ship going round in a circle and apt to vanish at any moment in a vortex of its own making. Let us then disentangle Bowsprit from Rudder by playing the game Carroll invented, called Doublets, according to which you can turn Head into Tail with the help of

Rule 10. 'Each word in the Chain must be formed from the preceding word by changing one letter in it, and one only. The substituted letter must occupy the same place, in the word so formed, which the discarded letter occupied in the preceding word, and all other letters must retain their places.'

('Doublets, A Word Puzzle', 1879)

I here append Carroll's first example:

HEAD
heal
teal
tell
tall
TAIL

Other examples that he gave were: Change BLACK to WHITE; Evolve MAN from APE; CARESS PARENT; WHY NOT?; and Prove RAVEN to be MISER.

RAVEN
riven
risen
riser
MISER

Why is a raven like a miser? Because three links join them. But, why *is* a raven like a miser? Picking up the echo of some very flat notes, let us turn this into a proper riddle:

If a raven is black because it utters notes, what colour is the man who hoards them?

This might also be put:

If a raven is black because it says what it means, what colour is a man who is mean with what he says?

Such a man might, without impropriety, be identified as the Banker in *The Hunting of the Snark*. He, like the raven, was dressed in black, though on being frightened by the Bandersnatch★ his waistcoat turned white. This answer, however, cannot be satisfactory, for clothes are a disguise under which Boojums of all kinds may lurk unsuspected. The real answer, indeed, is usually censored, for it has to do with an alchemical transformation of something leaden first into the form of BABY and lastly into GOLD. It is done by the Oedipus in us putting his end in his beginnings and finding himself, so to speak, snarked. This, said Carroll in yet another of his afterthoughts, is a word composed of 'Snail' at the beginning and 'Shark' at the end. No prizes are offered to name the complex

---

'he Bandersnatch also begins with a B and perhaps should be regarded , the 11th in the series rather than the Boojum. The various lessons taught in the *Snark* would then end with a lunatic Bank Holiday, while the question f what happens on the 12th would be left to the Boojum.

that arises when a certain kind of symbol has its tail bitten off by the mouth of another kind of symbol: for we must hold on first principles that psychoanalysis is included in Nonsense and not vice versa. Whether the same can be said of Alchemy is another matter, which we need not discuss. We can, however, remark that while the end of Alchemy is to transform lead into gold, the beginning of Nonsense is in turning guilt into letters,* often in an alliterative retort.

Alchemy begins with an A. So does Alliteration. So, though nothing is proved thereby, do

Alice
Adventures
Answers
Afterthoughts
Attitudes

for Carroll did not put them into a regular series. We therefore cannot apply to them the Duchess's moral, which can stand as

Rule 11. 'Take care of the sense, and the sounds will take care of themselves.'

This is known as telling a story, and the rule for that is

Rule 12. 'Begin at the beginning, and go on till you come to the end; then stop.'

For if you start at the end, you can take care of the sounds only by not bothering about the sense (the exception to this, of course, being an afterthought). This keeps the Boojum away, and is called playing Doublets. Another game with the same effect is called Syzygies, or word chains.

Rule 13. 'A Chain should be written as in the Example to Def. 3. It does not matter which given word is placed at the top. Any number of alternative Chains may be sent in.'**

Example to Def. 3
If the given words are 'walrus' and 'carpenter' (the Problem might be stated in the form '*Introduce* Walrus *to* Carpenter'), the following Chain would be a solution to the Problem:—

---

* When the verdict was called for, the Jury declined,
    As the word was so puzzling to spell;

The word was of course 'GUILTY', which the Snark had only to pronounce.

** This game was published by *Vanity Fair* in 1879, and set as a Competition; hence the last sentence.

WALRUS
(rus)
peruse
(per)
harper
(arpe)
CARPENTER

This gets a score of 18 points by Carroll's reckoning, but one of o if you want to know Why Walrus? Why Carpenter? All we know from Carroll is that it is possible to turn CARPENTER into BARONET without affecting the metre of the poem in which he figures. You can also turn WALRUS into VULTURE, and CARPENTER into HUSBANDMAN, as some Oxford students did in a parody to which LEWIS CARROLL was made to sign himself as LOUISA CAROLINE. The poem has to do with examinations, and the Vulture is there because he plucks his prey – an allusion to tradesmen being allowed to pluck at the Proctor's gown when he gave degrees, if the candidate had run up too many debts in town. The Husbandman supports himself by the use of the Plough. And in that parody we find – happy discovery – that the men who sit for their examinations

> Wrote with all their might,
> But, though they wrote it all by rote,
> They could not write it right.

The parody thus shows one way of dealing with Carroll's Riddle, and it is noteworthy that he himself passed the method by.* It was perhaps too simple for his taste: for when *he* parodied READING and WRITING he made the Mock Turtle come up with REELING and WRITHING, no doubt as symptoms of raving. But is there also a Boojum involved? Presumably, as we can see if we pose the question, When is a w not sounded?

Our first piece of evidence is to be found in the code Carroll made up for his use when trying to solve problems at night, without the use of pencil and paper. It allowed him to turn a numerical answer into words, which he found easier to remember in the morning.

---

*But only in *Wonderland*, for in *The Vision of the Three T's* we find this rousing verse:

> Here's to the Censors, who symbolize Sense,
>   Just as Mitres incorporate Might, Sir!
> To the Bursar, who never expands the expense!
>   And the Readers, who always do right, Sir!

51

| 1 | 2 | 3 | 4 | 5 | 6 | 7 | 8 | 9 | 0 |
|---|---|---|---|---|---|---|---|---|---|
| b | d | t | f | l | s | p | h | n | z |
| c | w | j | q | v | x | m | k | g | r |

He explained the correlations thus:

1. b and c, the first two consonants of the alphabet.
2. d from duo, w from two.
3. t from tres, the other may wait awhile. (The empty place is filled by j, which has no use elsewhere.)
4. f from four, q from quattuor.
5. l and v are the Roman symbols for fifty and five.
6. s and x from six.
7. p and m from septem.
8. h from huit, and k from okto.
9. n from nine; and g because it is so like 9.
0. z and r from zero.

And here is how the code can be used:

When a word has been found, whose last consonants represent the number required, the best plan is to put it as the last word of a rhymed couplet, so that, whatever other words in it are forgotten, the rhyme will secure the only really important word.

Now suppose you wish to remember the date of the discovery of America, which is 1492; the '1' may be left out as obvious; all we need is '492'.

Write it thus

| 4 | 9 | 2 |
|---|---|---|
| f | n | d |
| q | g | w |

and try to find a word that contains 'f' or 'q', 'n' or 'g', 'd' or 'w'. A word soon suggests itself – 'found'.

The poetic faculty must now be brought into play: and the following couplet will soon be evolved:

'Columbus sailed the world around
Until America was FOUND.'

(Collingwood, *Life and Letters*, pp. 268–9)

Pausing for a moment in honour of the ingenuity through which, when a word has been FOUND it is the one you were looking for to remind you of the date of the finding of America, we may note some peculiarities about the code. Collingwood, for instance, has

$$7$$
$$p$$
$$m$$

whereas the Ms note published by Weaver (*Scientific American*, April 1956, 194:4) gives

$$7$$
$$m$$
$$p.$$

The change may have been made by Carroll to go with the order of the consonants in 'septem', though the original shows he first followed the alphabetical order. This presumably explains

$$5$$
$$l$$
$$v$$

though it would have been logical to write

$$5$$
$$v$$
$$l$$

to preserve the order of magnitude of these letters as Roman numerals. The reason for his choice may perhaps be found in the fact that there are no vowels in the code. These, of course, are used to make words out of the consonants which stand for numbers, while also being used to give sense to two of the correlations, under 6 and 0. (The explanation for 0, however, is not as ingenious as it deserves to be – it might better be stated, Put an e between z and r and add zero.) If we added vowels to the l and v of 5, we can get two of Carroll's favourite words, LOVE and LIVE: and we know from *Sylvie and Bruno* that it is an easy matter to reverse LIVE so that it becomes EVIL. The vowels might also be placed amongst the consonants to make VILE: and this is as good a reason as any for not listing the code as

$$5$$
$$v$$
$$l.$$

Be this as it may, the exigencies of wit are quite ignored with the explanation for

$$2$$
$$d$$
$$w.$$

For, while there is certainly a w in two, as there is a p and an m in 'septem', what is a w but a Doubled U?

We shall return to this later. Meanwhile, the temptation to solve the Riddle by a simplified use of the code is great, even though the Riddle was first published in 1862, and the code in 1888. Following Carroll's remark on another matter, however, 'we are encouraged to do so by Mrs. Malaprop's advice: "Let us not anticipate the past; let all our retrospections be to the future", and by the fact that our family motto is *"Respiciendo prudens"*.' ('Misch-Masch', 1855.) (It was, actually, *'Respice et Resipice'*, and the family crest the head of Janus.) If we yield to temptation, therefore, a mathematical equation appears, proving that the spoken word can be remembered without writing it down at a desk.

$$\text{Does raven} = \text{writing} - \text{desk}?$$
$$\text{Yes: because} \quad 0 \quad = 2 \quad -2$$

This shows talent, though certainly exerted in the wrong direction. Let us try another answer to the question, When is a w not sounded?, namely: When you are caught in a self-contradiction that tails off into nothing.

'Give your evidence; and don't be nervous, or I'll have you executed on the spot.' Very well: as long as we keep in mind that the King who uttered these words later made a remark that was greeted with a dead silence, and had to break it by saying, in an offended tone, 'It's a pun!' Let us incarnate the w in the Tweedle brothers, and see what happens. 'To tweedle is to produce a succession of shrill musical notes, to whistle or pipe', says the *Oxford Companion to Literature*. 'The original contest is between the sounds of high and low-pitched musical instruments', and the original contestants were Handel and Buononcini, in 1720. The onlookers found it impossible to make a distinction between their skills, and John Byron wrote:

> Strange all this Difference should be
> Twixt Tweedle-dum and Tweedle-dee!

Tweedledum and Tweedledee lived in a Wood, and if you think they're Wax-Works, you ought to pay; for they weren't made to be looked at for nothing. 'Nohow!' And of course, 'Contrariwise'. You mustn't begin Wrong by pointing at them and saying 'First Boy!' and then 'Next Boy!', but say How d'ye do and shake hands – Dum's right hand and Dee's left to be precise – according to Tenniel's illustration, that is. Then it's time for poetry, with the Walrus and the Carpenter, and a sight of the Red King dreaming of them all, which raises the question of whether Alice would be Real if he Woke. A thunder-cloud forms while the brothers are getting ready

to fight over a Rattle. 'And how fast it comes! Why, I do believe it's got wings! It's the crow!' and the double You takes to its heels and is out of sight in a moment.

The alliterations here are, admittedly, infrequent, but the counterpoint of r- w- r- w- is suggestive when we return to the first time that the w was invisible, at the Tea-party. It will be remembered that a series of alliterations led up to the Riddle, in which r-s, v-s and w-s were permuted under the influence of the vowel sound 'i'. Dare we say, after pondering this evidence with a mind attuned to Nonsense, that a w is not sounded when a riddle begins with a y?★

The method in this madness depends on the fact that w and y share the distinction of being pronounced as consonants, as vowels, or as diphthongs, according to their context. This makes it natural for y to be pronounced as though it started with a w; and it is w which we must now investigate in its relations with r.

It is no great matter to turn r into w – in Victorian times, for instance, it would not have been thought wrong for a dandy to say 'wong'. It can also be turned into a z- or j- sound, as in the French transformation of 'chaire' into 'chaise'. Ernest Jones, in *On the Nightmare* (1910), has suggested that the r is 'lisped' because its

---

★As far as the Riddle is concerned, it will have flown away: for we must remember not only that Y is a raven, but that Y, it has wings. Carroll used this ploy in a letter to Ethel Arnold where, after the word 'affectionately' he adds: '(The long tail to the "Y" is to emphasise the question, "Y should I be affectionate?")' (Ethel Arnold, 'Reminiscences of Lewis Carroll', *Windsor Magazine*, vol. 71, 1930.)

sound is often associated with anger and fear, and that polite society deems it uncivil to express these emotions openly. But how is it then that the traditional pronunciation of 'wrong' is 'rong', and why does the word bear the marks of its having originally been pronounced w-rong? The combination of w- and r- must have a semantic function, which can be discovered if we examine other words beginning with wr-, thus: *w-rap*; *w-rath*, and its relatives *w-rist*, *w-rithe*, *w-ry*, *w-rest* and perhaps *w-riggle*; *w-reak*, and its relatives *w-reck*, *w-retch*, and the metathetical *urge*; *w-rench*, cousin to *w-ring*, *w-rangle*, *w-rinkle*, *w-rong* and the metathetical *worry*; and *w-rite*. When the w- is pronounced with r- in these words, the effect is of the sound worrying at the sense and giving it a turn. An appeal to the dictionary confirms this onomatopoeic insight. Thus 'worry' is defined by Chambers as 'to tear with the teeth; (Scot.) to devour ravenously', while under 'scribe' in Partridge's *Origins. A short etymological dictionary of modern English* we find: 'The basic idea is "to scratch", hence "to scratch characters upon bark or wax", hence "to write"', and he advises the reader to compare the like semantics of 'write', 'grammar' and 'graph'. As for 'wrath', Partridge gives the word the basic meaning of 'crooked', a word he uses to define other roots which express 'turning'.

We need not go into the etymological relations that exist between wr-, gr- and scr-, but focus rather on the w. We note that it, too, can be lisped into v (which Germans pronounce as f) or dropped altogether: for which Sam Weller is our vitness in pronouncing *woman* ''ooman'. (The same can happen to a y, incidentally: in *Sylvie and Bruno* Carroll records Bruno as saying ''Oo' for *you*.) We may suspect from this that a lisped or elided w is a proof of that kind of difficulty that babies experience in pronouncing two vowels without an intermediate consonant, or two consonants without an intermediate vowel.

And yet, what noise do children make when they cry?

> '*Speak roughly to your little boy,*
> *And beat him when he sneezes:*
> *He only does it to annoy,*
> *Because he knows it teases.*'
> CHORUS
> '*Wow! Wow! Wow!*'

This most primitive of diphthongs thus starts life as a complaint. Experience tells us that the complaint uttered by a baby is generally treated as a question to be answered by its mother, and etymology confirms this. The interrogative words that in English start with a w parallel the Latin ones that start with a q; and since they are interrogative, the place to find their meaning is under *query*. Partridge's *Origins* is again our informant. The word derives from Latin *quaere*; 'perh. it is akin to L queri, to utter plaintive cries, hence to complain, and, if that be so, it is prob akin to "to wheeze" (hence the n), ME *whesen*, which derives from or is, at the least, akin to ON *hvaesa*, to hiss, itself related to Skt *svasiti*, he breathes audibly, sighs, snorts.'

Here then is a phonetic Boojum issuing from the Boojum as child. Where it does not turn into a v, the w may disappear altogether; it can also, for much the same reasons, appear instead of an r. In words beginning with wr-, but pronounced r-, the w sound is evidently the sign that the speaker may betray his childishness by lisping, and it is therefore muted in favour of the adult and aggressive r. This tells us that w is the weak form of r, and r the strong form of w; hence the wr- sound gains its semantic function from the struggle between an easy and a difficult vocal operation. The sense of the operation is of course lost when the w is muted, but the fact that the resultant r- sound can be lisped shows us that the opposition between the two still has force.

Let us now return to the point we started from. We began by enquiring into its *locus standi* with the question: When a circular argument is snarked, on what is it supported? We took the Boojum to serve our turn here, and it turned out to be something that it is impossible not to think of by an effort of will, and to possess the secret of such verbal transformations as that of a w into an r. We concluded by observing that the opposition between these two is one between weakness and strength, between silence and speech.

We have also made out that in Carroll this opposition takes the form of a quarrel (which, being querulous, also derives from 'quaere'). We can therefore find the *locus standi* of our point in legal terms, its herald being the White Rabbit. His initials are those that give force to the Riddle by inversion, and he is the one who cries out 'Silence in the court!' during the Trial scene. Here then is our answer: the *locus standi* of our point is that of a mute, defined in this context as 'one who refuses to plead' – as it must refuse, since it rests its case on a matter that is not allowed.

What is the case? We have already described it phonetically, by noting that the Riddle is invented when the terms of an alliterative series change partners under the influence of the vowel sound 'i'. If we are to read our answer out of this, we need only capitalise the letter to see it as the obvious admonishment, 'if I were you . . .' Of course, it turns into something quite different in the accusative case, which it does when the other pronoun comes first: and the result of that is for 'mute' to become 'mutual', as we shall indeed find.

The reader may still wish to have an expert opinion on the *locus* *standi* of a mute.* Let us then call back Wittgenstein and examine him on his statement, 'Whereof one cannot speak, thereof one must be silent.' In true Carrollian spirit, these words in his Preface are quoted from the very end of the *Tractatus* itself. But though the sentence is memorable enough, it is only in the original German that the poetic faculty exemplifies its meaning – which it does by letting the r of speech give way to the w of silence. Since this faculty was already at work in the sentence immediately preceding, we shall quote it also. The English goes: 'He must surmount these propositions; then he sees the world rightly.' (This, of course, is the opinion we have asked for.) The two sentences in German, suitably arranged to show their poetic character, run thus:

> Er muss diese Sätze überwinden;
> dann sieht er die Welt richtig.
>
> Wovon man nicht sprechen kann,
> darüber muss man schweigen.

The permutation of sounds in these two quasi-couplets produces a fine effect, which students of harmony might well study with profit. However, Wittgenstein is Wittgenstein, and Carroll is Carroll; so let us take advantage of the melodious close Wittgenstein has afforded us by having an intermission, though Carroll must be allowed to lower the curtain himself.

> Then that concludes our present interview; so we will meet again when you have reviewed my Modern Rivals one by one. If you had any slow music handy, I would vanish to it; as it is – –

*Vanishes without slow music.*
End of Act One

(C. L. Dodgson, *Euclid and His Modern Rivals*, 1879)

. . . . . . . . .

---

*Its Nonsense standing is best told in the form of a riddle: if you stop me being mute, what sound do I make? Chambers provides the answer: '*ut, n.* a syllable representing the first note of the scale, now generally superseded by *do.*'

# The surd

Where have we got to? *Where* in German is *wo* (pronounced vo); in Welsh is *cw*; in Latin, *qua* and in Greek, *pou*. These changes exemplify the linguistic difference between what are called the P-Celts and the Q-Celts, who use one of these two letters at the expense of the other. Grimm's Law tabulates other differences which occur when passing from Latin to Romance languages: thus Latin r turns into Romance d or l. If we likewise spell out some of the changes rung out of our discussion of the Riddle, this is the result:

| | | |
|---|---|---|
| r | d | l |
| r | w | z/j |
| w | v | f |
| wh | qu | p |
| wh | sv | hv |
| wr | scr | gr |
| wr | r | |
| w | — | |

The w thus obeys the definition given in Chapter 2 of *The Dynamics of a Parti-cle*: 'A SURD is a radical whose meaning cannot be exactly ascertained. This class comprises a very large number of particles.'

That the radical originally in question was W. E. Gladstone need not detain us. Let us rather go to the dictionary for a further definition of *surd*: '*adj.* (*obs.*) deaf: (*obs.*) senseless: (math.) irrational: (*phon.*) voiceless. – n. an irrational quantity: a voiceless consonant.' (Chambers.)

A surd is thus irrational, or voiceless or, as we have deduced from the Riddle, both. We have, however, seen that there can be good reasons for the w to be voiceless, especially when it meets up with an r; and we can state the more obvious of these as a chiasmus:

> It is wong to be rude;
> It is worrying to lisp.

If the reader wonders how anyone might escape from this predicament, he might conclude that Silence Is Golden. But what, we must ask, is the prime matter from which this gold is transmuted?

Chapter IV

# The coupling

Euclid left us with the promise that he would meet us again when his modern rivals had been reviewed, and shortly before I announced the future development of 'mute' into 'mutual'. Nonsense demands that both operations be carried out simultaneously, and this can only be done by a revolutionary instrument we must now lay our hands on. First, however, we shall search for the rivals in Carroll himself, which is no great matter: their tracks are already in the *Dynamics*, in Definition IV of its second chapter.

A COUPLE consists of a moving particle, raised to the degree M.A., and combined with what is technically called 'a better half'. The following are the principal characteristics of a Couple: (1) It may be easily transferred from point to point. (2) Whatever *force of translation* was possessed by the uncombined particle (and this is often considerable), is wholly lost when the Couple is formed. (3) The two forces constituting the Couple habitually *act in opposite directions*.

We now need to find two rivals coupled into a surd, remembering that the class of surds comprises a very large number of particles. The obvious candidate is the Snark, formed out of a slow slimy snail and a rough, rapid, ravenous shark. Snarks being many,

> . . . It next will be right
> To describe each particular batch:
> Distinguishing those that have feathers, and bite,
> From those that have whiskers, and scratch.

Two candidates immediately offer themselves: the Jubjub bird, whose name implies that it repeats a word until its meaning lies in shreds;* and the Bandersnatch, who caused its victim the Banker

---

*It does so by means of its voice, that exactly recalls to mind 'A pencil that squeaks on a slate' in the Fit of the *Snark* entitled 'The Beaver's Lesson'. The original owner of this beast is to be found in 'The Palace of Humbug' (1855):

And one, a dotard grim and gray,
Who wasteth childhood's happy day
In work more profitless than play.

Whose icy breast no pity warms,
Whose little victims sit in swarms
And slowly sob on lower forms.

to faint from its larcenies. The archaeology of these two creatures takes us back to the *Alices*, where we have flamingoes and mustard on the one hand, which both bite, their moral being that 'Birds of a feather flock together'; and perhaps cats on the other, which according to Alice will eat a little bird as soon as look at it. But then there is also the White Rabbit with his whiskers, and the White King who turned cold to the end of the whiskers he did not have and scratched notes into his memorandum book; and of course the raven itself, which sports whiskers, and is like a writing-desk – because, obviously, of its inky feathers, though this spoils the symmetry.

It is not easy to follow this trail further, because it shows only too clearly how easy it can be to get transferred from point to point. How about characteristic (2), the force of translation? To see what happens to this when a Couple is formed, let us recombine Jubjub and Bandersnatch. We then have the Jabberwock, which had jaws, claws and whiskers (at least, Carroll did not object to Tenniel drawing them in); but it has scales instead of feathers, and its claws are specifically said to catch rather than to scratch. Because of these defects, what has happened to the force of translation is remarkable.

> '*Twas brillig, and the slithy toves*
> *Did gyre and gimble in the wabe:*
> *All mimsy were the borogoves,*
> *And the mome raths outgrabe.*

Occult meanings come thick and fast, though we look in vain for a word beginning with wr-. Instead, the Jabberwock whiffles, and the idea of its movement is elsewhere apportioned between br- and gr-, g- and w-, a t- or two and some lisped j-s, f-s, and v-s. Now, we might jump to the conclusion that, as Jabberwocky was originally written in reverse so that it could only be read in a looking-glass,★ one of the functions of the glass is to separate w from r. In support of this we could point to the fact that the chess pieces in *Looking-glass* separate the two letters by being White and Red ones, rather than White and Black. But this cannot be the proper solution, for

---

★I may as well put on record here a fairly appropriate reason for thinking that the Riddle can be answered 'Because Poe wrote on both', as Sam Loyd suggested. It is based on the entry dated June 30, 1892, in Carroll's diaries: 'Invented what I think is a *new* kind of riddle. A Russian had three sons. The first, Rab, became a lawyer; the second Ymra, became a soldier; and the third became a sailor. What was his name?'

Since y is in the van again, here is my reason, embodied in this kind of riddle. 'If writing produces no less than Jabberwocky when seen in a looking-glass, what more does raven say when spoken backwards?'

# STANZA OF ANGLO-SAXON POETRY.

> TWAS BRYLLYG, AND Yᵉ SLYTHY COVES
> DID GYRE AND GYMBLE IN Yᵉ WABE:
> ALL MIMSY WERE Yᵉ BOROGOVES;
> AND Yᵉ MOME RATHS OUTGRABE.

This curious fragment reads thus in modern characters:

> TWAS BRYLLYG, AND THE SLYTHY TOVES
> DID GYRE AND GYMBLE IN THE WABE:
> ALL MIMSY WERE THE BOROGOVES;
> AND THE MOME RATHS OUTGRABE.

The meanings of the words are as follows:

BRYLLYG. (derived from the verb to BRYL or BROIL.) "the time of broiling dinner, ie the close of the afternoon"

SLYTHY. (compounded of SLIMY and LITHE). "smooth and active"

TOVE. a species of Badger. They had smooth white hair, long hind legs, and short horns like a stag. lived chiefly on cheese

GYRE verb (derived from GYAOUR or GIAOUR, "a dog") "to scratch like a dog"

GYMBLE (whence GIMBLET) to screw out holes in anything

WABE (derived from the verb to SWAB or SOAK) "the side of hill" (from its being soaked by the rain)

MIMSY (whence MIMSERABLE and MISERABLE) "unhappy"

BOROGOVE An extinct kind of Parrot. They had no wings, beaks turned up, and made their nests under sun-dials, lived on veal

MOME (hence SOLEMOME, SOLEMONE and SOLEMN). "grave"

RATH. A species of land turtle. Head erect, mouth like a shark, the fore legs curved out so that the animal walked on it's knees, smooth green body. lived on swallows and oysters.

OUTGRABE. past tense of the verb to OUTGRIBE. (it is connected with the old verb to GRIKE or SHRIKE, from which are derived "shriek" and "creak".) "squeaked"

Hence the literal English of the passage is:
"It was evening, and the smooth active badgers were scratching and boring holes in the hill side: all unhappy were the parrots, and the grave turtles squeaked out."

There were probably sun-dials on the top of the hill, and the "borogoves" were afraid that their nests would be undermined. The hill was probably full of the nests of "raths", which ran out squeaking with fear on hearing the "toves" scratching outside. This is an obscure, but yet deeply affecting relic of ancient Poetry.

Croft 1855          Ed

in none of the poems contained in the two *Alices* is there a word beginning with wr-, and there are only two in the whole of the *Snark*. Carroll's prose, on the other hand, contains a fair number. It seems rather that when a Couple is translated into poetry, the surd moves away from the w and settles elsewhere.

We can prove this by imitating the hero of Jabberwocky, who executes the movement we have imputed to the surd by cutting the monster's head off. We shall therefore take vorpal sword in hand and, snicker-snack, go 'One, two! One, two!' according to the third characteristic of a Couple. This states that its constituent forces act in opposite directions – a matter also referred to in Definition II of the *Dynamics*:

> PLAIN ANGER is the inclination of two voters to one another, who meet together, but whose views are not in the same direction.

Let us therefore try to reconstruct the debate that produces plain anger, and so determine the law of the motion. This is not hard, since a motion is in fact a legal term – it means appealing to court for a ruling on what is incidental to the progress of a cause, and not on its issue. The issue for us will then be the Riddle, and the incident we are dealing with has to do with the movement of a surd.

We shall assume that the Riddle is not a piece of poetry, largely on the evidence of the flat notes of its fairly appropriate Answer. We have already had some trouble with it where it comes to a raven never being *put* with its wrong end in front. We tried to get over the difficulty by putting a question instead, and now it must be time to put it to the vote.

Very well: the jury is already assembled, and has received its instructions from the Queen of Hearts: 'Sentence first – verdict afterwards.' The briefest of cross-examinations (which the King asked the Queen to take on for him, since it quite made his forehead ache) shows that the Answer obeys the instructions to the letter. It consists of two parts, and as the part which is never put with its wrong end in front comes last, that must be the verdict: the sentence is therefore in front, delivered in a few very flat notes. Our ruling on the law governing a motion must then be, that if the verdict were put the other way round, the sentence would be in verse.★

Indeed, 'this portentous movement has already assumed the dimensions of a Revolution!' as the Lord Chancellor said in *Sylvie and Bruno*. For having previously turned 'movement' into 'motion',

---

★However, when a Couple is not engaged in legal affairs, the matter is best seen as a proportion: verse is to prose as pros are to cons, the whole being suitably represented by the injunction 'Converse'.

we must now go one step further and turn it into 'moment'. This is already heralded in the *Dynamics* as 'MOMENT is the product of the mass into the velocity' and, in confirmation of the toves' liking for sundials, '*no moment is ever lost, by fully enlightened Particles*'.

Where does this lead to but the mome raths? We have two definitions of these creatures, for Carroll wrote the first verse of 'Jabberwocky' in 1855, adding a gloss of the 'Anglo-Saxon' terms, and the other verses in 1867 as a parody of his cousin Menella Smedley's poem, 'The Shepherd of the Giant Mountains', afterwards inserted in *Looking-glass* with glosses provided by Humpty Dumpty. The first version states that 'mome' means 'grave', curiously evolved from 'solemn', and that a rath is 'A species of land turtle. Head erect, mouth like a shark, the forelegs curved out so that the animal walked on its knees, lived on swallows and oysters.' For Humpty Dumpty a mome rath was a kind of green pig 'from home'. How this transformation may have occurred leads one to talk of many things, the most obvious being whether pigs have wings. They have indeed, for that is how they get mome. Tenniel illustrated them accurately enough, with curly tails like those of the toves, great flapping ears, and mouths open in that squealing grunt which is an 'outgribing'; and one of them looks as if it were about to take off backwards. That, of course, is the direction pigs fly in, as Partridge tells us in his *Dictionary of Slang and Unconventional English*: 'pigs fly, when. Never: coll. C.17–20. Withals in his Dict defines *terra volat* as "pigs flie in the ayre with their tayles forward".'

We shall take a rath to be this kind of pig. It is therefore the opposite of a raven that is never put with its wrong end in front – though also strangely like one if we extend the sense of 'raven' to 'ravenous', with the sharkish mouth of the rath ('He eats like a shark!' as the Vice-Chancellor said of Baron Doppelgeist in *Sylvie and Bruno*) reminding one that a pig is considered to be a pig because it eats like one (and as though no moment should be lost).

Two things follow, if a rath's tail is in front. We should first alter 'mome raths' to 'rath momes', understanding 'rath' as 'quick, eager, early' – as in Milton's 'rathe primroses' – and 'mome' as the ultimate abbreviation of 'movement'. The whole then signifies a moment so brief it is out of time ('I know I have to beat time when I learn music,' said Alice). But this transposition will hold only if the rath – whose tail is in a position to act as a corkscrew when it flies backwards – can also bore holes like a gimlet when it walks forwards.

It can. 'Ask our men of science: they will tell you that any German book must needs surpass an English one.' (*The Vision of the Three T's*.) Turning therefore to Johannes Meisenheimer's *Geschlecht und Geschlechter* (1921, p. 242), we read of the pig that 'the long and

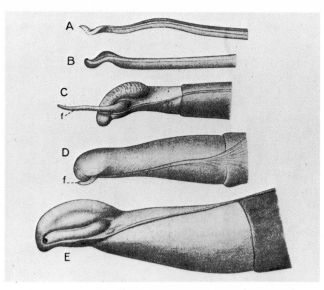

*'Penisformen verschiedener artiodaktyler Huftiere: A von Sus, B von Tragelaphus, C von Capra, D von Poephagus, E von Bos'*

slender copulatory member has a left-hand twist at its pointed end, and has the appearance of a corkscrew on account of the spiral having almost one and a half turns' (See A above).

The first quatrain of 'Jabberwocky' thus gives us the implement by which one can couple in opposite directions, namely a green pig. Wielded in the forward direction, when it has a left-hand twist, it will produce more pigs;* but when applied backwards (which is said never to happen only because it occurs out of time) it will outgribe with the portentous message often found on sundials: 'Time Flies.'

Let us recapitulate. When a Couple is formed, the force of translation possessed by the uncombined particle (in our case, a w) is wholly lost. It can, however, be recovered if these rivals are translated into verse, with the result that the surd moves away from the w and settles inside a portmanteau. As Humpty Dumpty tells us, a portmanteau has two meanings packed into one word; but we have found that 'packed' is a euphemism. The two meanings are screwed together.

---

*It is useful to remember that a pig has long been slang for a sixpence, which can be saved in a piggy-bank; and also for a police-officer, the more so for our purposes if he is not on his beat.

Here then we have our revolutionary instrument – a coupling device that fulfils the two requirements of including the sense of 'rival' and, by suppressing 'mutiny', of developing 'mute' into 'mutual'. If we think about this ('"I've a right to think," said Alice sharply. . . . "Just about as much right," said the Duchess, "as pigs have to fly"'), we cannot escape from dealing with the portentous matter by which a movement becomes a revolution, and moment the product of the mass into the velocity. Luckily, it has a name which means the shape it is – Humpty Dumpty.

Who is Humpty Dumpty? Taylor, faced by this question in *The White Knight*, makes an illuminating quotation from Fechner, the German experimental psychologist (1801–87): 'But I consider the world as a fat hen, of which philosophy is just a wind egg.' Humpty Dumpty is indeed the Egg of Nonsense, though not laid by any feathered fowl. Oh, no indeed! Let us just consider his cravat, which is so difficult to tell from a belt. This was a present from the White King and Queen – not a birthday one, that you may expect only once a year, but an unbirthday one, which you might get on 364 days. But how do you give a birthday present to an egg? It is the other way round: the egg is tied with a ribbon as a present on the day that gives birth to what it contains. This is of course Easter Sunday, the egg's parent being the March Hare: but since this is a moveable feast, governed by the phases of the moon, the present of an egg cannot be expected, *pace* Humpty Dumpty, on any one of 364 days, but only on one between March 22 and April 25.

We may find confirmation for this in the obvious place, namely Carroll's 'An Easter Greeting to Every Child who Loves "Alice"'. Having delivered a religious message, he writes:

> Are these strange words from the writer of such tales as 'Alice'? And is this a strange letter to find in a book of nonsense? It may be so. Some perhaps may blame me for thus mixing together things grave and gay; others may smile and think it odd that any one should speak of solemn things at all, except in church and on a Sunday: but . . . I do not believe God means us thus to divide life into two halves . . .★

No: according to Carrollian logic, He expects us to pack everything into a portmanteau, the grave and the gay forming a single egg. Humpty Dumpty is the professor of this subject, the master of words, his poem about fishes telling us what school he belonged to – probably the same one attended by the Mock Turtle, who

---

★ This was printed as a small pamphlet in 1876 and first inserted in copies of *The Hunting of the Snark*, being later reprinted as part of the 1887 edition of *Looking-glass*.

(though originally a calf) became fish-like when drowned in tears of frustration. But there is certainly no evidence that the chapter in which Humpty Dumpty figures was written to celebrate Easter. Plainly, it was written to celebrate 'Jabberwocky'.

We do not know the exact date in 1855 that Carroll wrote the first verse of 'Jabberwocky', but we may find the event it celebrates by consulting Hone's *Every Day Book*. This was found in Carroll's library after his death, and there are many indications that he had read it. The most obvious of these occurs as the entry for January 17 (ten days before his birthdate), which deals at length with the Temptation of St Anthony. The illustration catches the eye at once: it is an engraving of the Temptation after a painting by Salvator Rosa, showing the saint grovelling on the earth, doing his best to ward off two unsightly demons. The larger demon is unmistakably

the original of the Jabberwock, and it seems clear that Carroll drew Tenniel's attention to the figure and liked the result so much that he wished to have it as the frontispiece to *Looking-glass*.

St Anthony's Temptation was, of course, a trial of faith, and its agents were nightmare figures. For the relevance of this to Carroll, we may quote the entry for his diary dated February 9, 1856:

> Query: When we are dreaming and, as often happens, have a dim consciousness of the fact and try to wake, do we not say and do things which in waking life would be insane? May we not then sometimes define insanity as an inability to distinguish which is the waking and which the sleeping life?

We have already noted that Carroll was plagued with 'unholy thoughts' at night, and that he would drive them away by feats of mental arithmetic. Since he himself did not go into particulars, we must leave the nature of these thoughts undetermined. What we can do, however, is to note what Carroll held to be an immediate cause of nightmares or, as he put it in 'Phantasmagoria', of the visit of the Knight-Mayor and Corporation. This personage 'goes about and sits on folk/That eat too much at night' – such things as eggs and bacon, lobster, duck and toasted cheese – and make indigestible Humpty Dumpties of themselves. They are then put to the trial and learn for themselves how, as Hone says, St Anthony 'is always represented by the old painters with a pig by his side'. (He is also represented by the letter 'T'.)

Hone also reminds us that in honour of St Anthony's power of curing pigs, '"they used in several places to tie a bell about the neck of a pig, and maintain it at the common charge of the parish" from whence came our English proverb of "Tantony pig"' – usually the feeblest of the litter. So we are back with our rath, who lives on such knight-mayorish things as swallows and oysters and who *outgribes*. Carroll made out that this was connected with the old verb to GRIKE or SHRIKE, from which are derived 'shriek' and 'creak', and thus meant 'to squeak'. This is likely enough: we have already noted the semantic equivalence of wr-, gr- and scr-, and the new variants shr- and cr- are welcome additions to the list. But it cannot be the whole story, for the transformation of k to b is phonologically unsound. True, it would let us find the original of 'outgrabe' as 'outgrake', with a corresponding alteration of 'wabe' (a long way before, and a long way behind, and a long way beyond) to 'wake', which is intriguing. It is more likely, however, that the b was originally a p, and that the word Carroll was making Nonsense of was GRIPE. (We find confirmation of this in the Gryphon, whose old name was Gripe, and who outgribed with occasional exclamations of 'Hjckrrh!')

To gripe means to grasp, hence can refer to severe spasmodic pains in the intestines. (The word is also used by sailors for a ship that is inclined to turn its head into the wind.) We shall see in due course the medicine Carroll used for this malady: here it allows us to give a curious meaning to 'mome'. First we must listen to Alice as she is falling down the rabbit-hole:

'I wonder if I shall fall right *through* the earth! How funny it'll seem to come out among the people that walk with their heads downwards! The antipathies, I think –'

It was of course to the Antipodes that the Snark sentenced the pig to be transported for life – the usual term of fourteen years being found, with a slight alteration, in the fine of £40 imposed on it at the same time. The relevance of all this to GRIPE can be found by making a somewhat disagreeable pun, namely that a rath is indeed 'from home' when sent to the colonies. 'Jabberwocky' allows us to bear this out, for though the poem is not punctuated by a single colon, there is a Tumtum★ tree in a tulgey wood beside which the hero stands in uffish thought after seeking the manxome foe. As for the sense of this last adjective, it is found if we practise the reversal we have found necessary with other Jabberwockian terms – the monster must be some manx, if its head is cut off before its tale is finished.

We have done something to elucidate the nature of a Couple, and it is now time to think a little about Anglo-Saxon, the putative language in which 'Jabberwocky' is written. The prose-speaker of this language is, of course, the Messenger, who gets into curious Attitudes as he skips along wriggling like an eel. I do not say this was the same eel that Father William balanced on his nose in *Wonderland* but we at least have a word beginning with wr-, applied to one of the members of the Tea-party, now in fancy dress. And William with its W brings to mind another R, in the afterthought about 'Jabberwocky' that Carroll prefaced to *The Hunting of the Snark*. Here is the passage:

> Supposing that, when Pistol uttered the well-known words –
> '*Under which king Bezonian? Speak or die!*'
> Justice Shallow had felt certain that it was either William or Richard, but had not been able to settle which, so that he could not possibly say either name before the other, can it be doubted that, rather than die, he would have gasped out 'Rilchiam!'

Rilchiam, indeed. This result of 'that rarest of gifts, a perfectly balanced mind', as the Preface goes on to say, allows us to record

Rule 14. *To save your life, hide it in a portmanteau*

before continuing on our way. For the Messenger's name was not William or Richard, but Haigha; and, as we have noted, his wrigglings make an alliterative series of being Happy and Hideous, while his bag contained Ham-sandwiches and Hay. What else is in it?

---

★ If the reader finds this allusion hard to stomach, he should turn to *The New Method of Evaluation as Applied to π* (1865), which deals with the religious and financial controversy then centering on Professor Jowett. Commenting on a proposal that Jowett should be eliminated *in toto*, Carroll remarks: 'The classical scholar need hardly be reminded that *toto* is the ablative of *tumtum*, and that this beautiful and expressive phrase embodied the wish that J should be eliminated by the compulsory religious examination.'

Given that there are two counters in a bag, as to which all that was originally known was that each was either black or white. Also given that the experiment has been tried, a certain number of times, of drawing a counter, looking at it, and replacing it; that it has been white every time; and that, as a result, the chance of drawing white is $\frac{a}{a+b}$. Also given that the same experiment is repeated $m$ times more, and that it continues to be white every time. What would then be the chance of drawing white?

The answer is: $\frac{2^m \cdot (a-b)+b}{2^m \cdot (a-b)+2b}$. There is thus a faint possibility that the Messenger will draw another letter out of his bag. Indeed, he has already done so, with the two slices of B and B that enclose the H. This sandwiching of two alliterative series does produce a Couple of a kind, but not one in which the constituents necessarily *act in opposite directions*. If this is to happen, it seems essential for the Couple to be formed under the influence of poetry, and while being translated into Anglo-Saxon. For only then do we get that unprecedented musical riddle of 'Jabberwocky' with its baggage of snark-like words.

As we have said, the personage incarnating the meaning of these portmanteaus is Humpty Dumpty, for it is he who explains how they are to be unpacked. Thus *slithy*, he says, means *lithe*★ and *slimy*. Do these act in opposite directions? To answer this we must ask what life they hide in their conjunction, as they must if Rule 14 is correct. For metre and rhyme alone, though certainly casting a spell upon words, cannot be expected to screw two words together unless they already have some hidden affinity. That this affinity can be betrayed by alliteration, however, is apparent from the noun that *slithy* qualifies: toves.

The first definition of *tove* which Carroll gave was: 'a species of Badger. They had smooth white hair, long hind legs, and short horns like a stag. Lived chiefly on cheese.' If that was the long and short of it, we should not be much advanced. But by the time Humpty Dumpty got at toves, they had turned into something like a badger, and something like a lizard, and something like a corkscrew; and they nested in the ground beneath sundials. I take this to be a more accurate definition, like the one Humpty Dumpty gave for *gyre* – 'to go round and round like a gyroscope' – in favour of the original gloss that derived the word from *giaour* (the Turks'

---

★According to M. C. F. Morris in *Yorkshire Folk Talk* (1892), 'to lithe' means to thicken anything boiled with flour, linseed, etc.

word for an infidel), with the meaning 'to scratch like a dog'. This is well enough: but the circular meaning given by him to gyre, the next word gimble, and the toves themselves nesting beneath the shadow of the rotating sun, tells us that the hidden meaning of the surd has now shown its hand to anyone who is watching.

We have already caught sight of this meaning, and how it manages to make a Couple from oppositely acting parts: it has to do with the orbital motion of a mass about a centre. If we focus on this we see, not just the egg of Humpty Dumpty, but the corkscrewed tove and its rath-like counterpart. (That 'rath' may also stand for 'wraith' is probable, but the proof must be left till Chapter IX.) For after Humpty Dumpty has shown who is master of such words, he recites his poem about fishes to Alice. In this appears yet another messenger – not Haigha, who wriggles, or Hatta, who is drinking tea again, but one who is very stiff and proud. Immediately after him the corkscrew reappears, to combine stiffness with wriggling.

The corkscrew makes its last appearance in Humpty Dumpty's hands when Alice has been Queened, in connection with thunder and hippopotamuses. The connection is hardly explained by the thunder being described as 'rolling round the room in great lumps', though this certainly entails the motion of a mass. The question of how something that lives in the earth beneath a sundial can be used to get thunder out of a hippopotamus, or both out of a room, is best answered by Humpty Dumpty's 'Impenetrability!'

This means, according to him, that we have had enough of that subject. However, since the subject was originally taught by Carroll's tutor, Professor Bartholomew Price, we shall give his explanation of the term: 'Matter exists in space and time: all matter, even the minutest particles, occupies space. No two particles of matter and, also, no two bodies can occupy the same space at the same time; this property of matter is called its *impenetrability*.' (Quoted in Taylor, p. 124.)

Is this property of matter also one of portmanteaus? Apparently not: because the elements which comprise them are not mutually exclusive, but mutually inclusive. And yet, as the logic of verbal portmanteaus shows, this mutuality depends on each element silencing a part of its character, so that they cease to move in opposite directions but are cemented together by a surd.

I use this verb in honour of a story written by Carroll in 1856, which he called 'Novelty and Romancement: A broken Spell.' Beginning with the words, 'I had grave doubts at first whether to call this passage of my life "A Wail", or "A Paean"', it soon has the hero going on a walk on Friday, the fourth of June, at half-past four p.m. (He was no doubt Carroll himself, since the fourth of June did fall on a Friday in 1856: the occasion presumably being the official birthday of George III, which was still held as an unofficial holiday long after he died.) He then sees a signboard bearing the word 'Romancement', and questions the mechanic in charge what the article was employed for. The mechanic answered: 'It would piece almost anything together, . . . and make it solider nor stone.'

This was a sentence difficult of interpretation. I thought it over a little, and then said, doubtfully, 'you mean, I presume, that it serves to connect the broken threads of human destiny? to invest with a – with a sort of vital reality the chimerical products of a fertile imagination?'

Imagine the hero's discomfiture when he sees the board next day, and finds that a gap has crept in between the n- and the -c . . .

If we transfer this hero to *Looking-glass*, several things become clear. We find him, stiff with armour and accoutred with fire-irons, saving Alice from distress – even though she complained, right at the beginning of the book, that he was a nasty Knight to come wriggling down amongst her chess pieces. (Two pages later he is sliding down the poker.) *He* knew a recipe for Roman Cement if anyone did: it was for a pudding he invented one day during the meat course, composed of blotting paper, gunpowder and sealing-wax. 'In time to have it cooked for the next course?' Alice enquired. 'Well, that *was* quick work.' 'Well, not the *next* course; no, certainly not the next *course*,' the Knight replied. Not even the next day.

What has all this to do with toves, and raths, and corkscrews, and

hippopotamuses? Some kind of answer can be given,★ but only by breaking

Rule 15. *When a dog (or a Red King, for that matter) is sleeping, let it lie.*

This rule is important, for we know that both the *Alices* are presented as dreams, with the last line of the envoi to *Looking-glass* maintaining that even 'Life, what is it but a dream?' It has also been claimed by another expert in this field that the main function of a dream is to secure the sleep of the subconscious. Indeed, if it is disturbed while pulling a rabbit out of a hat during the dog days, who knows how rabid the subconscious will become? We shall therefore try to avoid the rude awakening of the dreamer by turning to Partridge's *Origins* for our summing up:

1.  *Stiff* comes from a root meaning 'to crowd together', and produces *costive*.
2.  *Wriggle* is akin to *wry*, from a root meaning 'crooked'. It gives us *rick*, a twist in the neck. The word *crick* can also be used for this, but it is said to be a thinning of *creak*, which derives from *croak*.
3.  'To twist' in Latin is *torquere*. This leads on the one hand to *retort*, via *tort*, a wrongful deed, which also gives *turd*; and on the other to *tortoise*, on account of its twisted legs. *Tautology*, however, comes from the Greek τὸ αὐτό, 'the same'.
4.  The opposite of 'twisted' in Latin is *rectus*, straight, right, which may have more than an accidental similarity to *rigid*. From it derives *rex*, *rector*, *regular*, *rule*, *right*, *rich* and *rectum*.
5.  *Screw* derives from Latin *scrofa*, a sow and hence a vulva, and is cognate with *scratch* and *scribe*. From *scrofa* we have *scrofula*, the King's Evil – but St Anthony's fire is *erysipelas*.

---

★ We cannot lose the opportunity of giving yet another kind of answer to the Riddle here, by converting raven and writing-desk to the nearly perfect anagram of 'Giant Screwdriver'.

# Chapter V

# Making the world go round

Polite society has always held that silence is golden concerning the matters dealt with in the last chapter, because it is in silence that they are sublimed. Nonsense deals with them by the use of a surd, and the process can take various forms: shutting a portmanteau on two words, or two meanings, is one of them; shutting Alice up like a telescope is another; cooking a third, the use of glue, cement or jam a fourth, and that of a screw a fifth. But since Nonsense is polite even in its rudeness, the results of the sublimation remain equivocal, for the absence that it enshrines makes it impossible to determine in the end whether 'I mean what I say' is the same as 'I say what I mean', or different, or both at the same time.

Victorian society was more polite than ours about such things, and the success of Carroll's Nonsense may partly be ascribed to its adumbration of forbidden topics with something that approaches jesuitical skill. Carroll can hardly have avoided being at the receiving end of such skill, as deployed by the propagators of the Oxford Movement: for in the year before *Wonderland* was published, namely 1864, Charles Kingsley (the brother of Henry, one of Carroll's best friends) published a pamphlet entitled 'What, then, does Dr. Newman mean?' in which the following passage occurs:

> How can I tell that I shall not be the dupe of some cunning equivocation, of one of the three kinds laid down as permissible by the blessed St. Alfonso de Liguori and his pupils even when confirmed with an oath, because 'then we do not deceive our neighbour, but allow him to deceive himself'? . . . It is admissible, therefore, to use words and sentences which have a double signification, and leave the hapless hearer to take which of them he may choose. What proof have I, then, that by 'I *mean* it! I never said it!' Dr. Newman does not signify, 'I did not say it, but I did [query, *not*?] mean it'?

The attitude of one sitting on this kind of fence is described by the White Knight, the Pudding inventor, in the last stanza of Carroll's Wordsworthian parody: and by it we may find what movement occurs when you have your cake and eat it.

> *'And now, if e'er by chance I put*
> *My fingers into glue,*
> *Or madly squeeze a right-hand foot*
> *Into a left-hand shoe,*
> *Or if I drop upon my toe*
> *A very heavy weight,*
> *I weep, for it reminds me so*
> *Of that old man I used to know . . .*
> *A-sitting on a gate.'*

Before we take up this matter, it is as well to know that Carroll invented the character of the White Knight largely to suit that of the speaker in the parody (letter to Brimsley Johnson, quoted in *The Diaries of Lewis Carroll*, edited by R. L. Green, 1953, p. 91). But the reason the speaker has for remembering the Aged Aged Man – whose name, it will be remembered, Carroll took to himself – suggests that the two of them are not different characters so much as the two faces of a single one. Now Janus, whose head appears on the Dodgson family crest, is the gate-keeper of the year, and therefore the guardian of the circularity of Time as measured by the cycles of the sun. Any stickler for detail must ask himself just where in this circle the guardian is to be placed, and Carroll was no exception. Indeed, the problem was the subject of the first DIFFICULTY he presented, when still a youth, in the family periodical 'The Rectory Umbrella':

> Supposing on Tuesday, it is morning in London; in another hour it would be Tuesday morning at the west of England; if the whole were land we might go on tracing Tuesday morning, Tuesday morning all the way round, till in 24 hours after Tuesday morning it is Wednesday morning. Where then in its passage round the earth, does the day change its name? where does it lose its identity?

This question can only be settled by arbitration, and was in fact so settled by the establishment of the International Date Line: largely, of course, on the prior claim of the Greenwich Meridian. In like fashion the White Knight and the Aged Aged Man are antipodal to each other, and if one sits on a gate to see the world go by (or round) the other is showing how the world does so.

Now, what does make the world go round? Is it
a) minding your own business – the Duchess's first suggestion?
b) love – her second one?
c) a corkscrew beneath a sundial?
d) squeezing a right-hand foot into a left-hand shoe?★

---

★ In the nursery, this action would result in a mome rath and the cry: 'Wee wee wee wee, I can't find my way home.'

The answer, of course, is that all of them are involved, even though the Duchess added that a) would make the world go round a deal faster than it does. We can note that d) and c) have much in common: both have a right-hand twist. How far a) and b) share a similar attitude may be deduced after we have put d) in front of a looking-glass, and seen the results:

| right | hand | foot | in | left  | hand | shoe |
|-------|------|------|----|-------|------|------|
| left  | foot | hand | in | right | foot | —    |

You can't deny the logic of this even if you tried with both hands, as the Red Queen said. But what is the missing word? Glue? or Glove?

Glove. Carroll always wore black and grey gloves, Isa Bowman recorded, whatever the weather. He also was noted to have an extreme horror of infection, so it is likely that he wore gloves as a hygienic measure. This would not at all contradict a more general assumption, that the wearing of gloves is the visible outward sign of minding one's own business. That this need not go with the inward spiritual grace implied, however, is suggested by the fact that although Carroll always wore a top hat, he never wore a top coat. Is this connected with minding one's own business? It certainly leads us into matters of possession, for we know that when the Hatter was told to take off his hat during the Trial, he replied 'It's not mine', and that the Baker did not mind the loss of his baggage containing his clothes because he had seven coats on when he came to hunt the Snark. He must have lost these one by one and Fit by Fit, like Ishtar disrobing at each of the seven gates of the Underworld, because at the end of the last Fit he vanished. If he had been wearing a top hat, perhaps he would only have been sent to prison. (That he was somehow also wearing three pairs of boots is a matter I shall leave for the moment.)

Let us then assume that Carroll's sartorial habits are a kind of anti-corkscrew, to hide the twist of c) and d). Isa Bowman recorded other traits in Carroll that show just how far-reaching this twist was, and provide physiognomic parallels to the Anglo-Saxon Attitudes we have so far noted. He suffered, for instance, from Housemaid's Knee, which made his movements singularly jerky and abrupt; he stuttered, especially on the letter P; he was deaf in his right ear as a result of infantile fever which was made worse by an attack of mumps when he was 17; and he had a curiously womanish face, 'in direct contradiction to his real character'. Alice Liddell said that 'he always held himself upright, as if he had swallowed a poker'; and others have remarked, that he held one shoulder higher than the other, that he had two profiles, took an unusual interest in literature dealing with epileptic fits, suffered from respiratory ailments (during which, no doubt, he wheezed), rheumatism and ague-like fevers, and migraines with castellation but without pain. ('Castellation' is the term for visions of battlemented forms, which often revolve.) He had poor vision in his right eye, and is generally supposed to have been left-handed though, as his biographer R. L. Green remarks, there is no direct evidence for this. However, several of his brothers and sisters tended to be left-handed, and his sister Louisa was definitely so. (She was as good a mathematician as he was, and he often consulted her on a difficult problem.) Nor may we overlook the fact that it was the left-hand bit of mushroom that made Alice grow taller, and the right-hand one shorter.

Together, these traits suggest that he also suffered from torticollis, and that they would have made a dreadfully ugly child.★ Here is how Alice handled the complication, in the shape of the handsome pig the child turned into:

> As soon as she made out the proper way of nursing it (which was to twist it up into a sort of knot, and then keeping tight hold of its right ear and left foot, so as to prevent its undoing itself), she carried it out into the open air.

We shall do the same, via a syllogistic riddle:

> If you are mad to put a right-hand foot into a left-hand shoe, and you are deaf because your left foot is in your right ear, what are you when you wear gloves on both hands?
> Answer: A Bachelor.★★

Proof: the letter Carroll wrote to Isa Bowman in reply to one of hers, in which she enclosed 'Sacksful of love and basketsful of kisses'. Carroll joyfully took the opportunity of turning these into gloves worn by kittens, which could only be taken off when mice were to be caught.

> But the moment they've caught the mice, they pop their gloves on again, because they know we can't love them without their gloves. For, you see, 'gloves' have got *love* inside them – there's none *outside*!! . . .

> Your loving old Uncle,
> C.L.D.

---

★ 'I wish you all success with your little boys – To me they are not an attractive race of beings (as a little boy, I was simply detestable).' (Letter to Mrs Richards, March 13, 1882.)

★★ Fittingly enough, this word originally signified a young knight; a knight-bachelor being one who is not a member of any order.

Carroll was her uncle only in a manner of speaking, and used the word for the good reason that the relation of uncle to niece is not direct but at one remove both down and sideways. This equivalent to the Knight's move in chess (which Alice described as a wriggle) gives a man the right to show such affection as he pleases to a girl without his motives being called into question; as long, of course, as he does not enter that area where the relationship is proscribed. That he must wear gloves of a kind in this situation goes without saying.

We may now return to our question, What makes the world go round? We have shown that d) and c) are fitting answers, and so are b) and a) as long as these are taken together. The conjunction is effected, not so much by a surd, as by a proportion: it can be expressed as, Gloves are to kittens as love is to kisses. There can be no doubt that this adds up to a protection against Passion in general, and against things which have whiskers, and scratch, in particular. But if these last are kittens, they are also Queens in the chess game. For the black kitten turns into the Red Queen, and the white one into the White Pawn that ends as Queen Alice. (It originally stood for another of Carroll's girl friends, who was too young to appreciate the moves of chess: but Alice was then happily immersed in learning them.)

Then there is the original White Queen, and the Queen of Hearts. As for the distinguishing traits of these queens, 'I pictured to myself the Queen of Hearts as a sort of embodiment of ungovernable passion – a blind and aimless Fury. The Red Queen I pictured as a Fury, but of another type; *her* passion must be cold and calm; she must be formal and strict, yet not unkindly; pedantic to the tenth degree, the concentrated essence of all governesses! Lastly, the White Queen seemed, to my dreaming fancy, gentle, stupid, fat and pale; helpless as an infant; and with a slow, maundering, bewildered air about her just *suggesting* imbecility . . .' ('"Alice" on the Stage'.)

We have already noted that Fury is the name of the dog in the Mouse's Tale, who prosecutes, judges and wishes to execute his victim – a curious choice of animal, one might think, since dogs are ratters while mousers are cats. Anyhow, it is likely that the Queen of Hearts was not a cat, for she certainly would not stand being looked at by one – did she not order the Cheshire Cat's head to be removed, though at the time it was not attached to a body? We must of course remember that the Mouse's Tale was told on an afternoon when it was raining cats and dogs, which would explain part of this quarrelsome rivalry.★ But the Red and White Queens are cats – at least, kittens – and here a question of age creeps in. For the White Queen is as helpless as the infant Pawn, while Alice has grown up sufficiently to be crowned at the end of the game. And

---

★The Mouse had its own quarrel with these animals, so that Alice finally had to allude to them by their initials. These are also the initials of Charles Dodgson, a fact that will be dealt with in its proper place. But we should also remember that cat and dog quarrels are matrimonial, as a re-reading of Definition IV of the *Dynamics* at the beginning of Chapter IV will show.

how did Carroll characterise her? 'Loving, first, and gentle; loving as a dog (forgive the prosaic simile, but I know no earthly love so pure and perfect), and gentle as a fawn – then courteous . . .'

What rules shall we apply to understand these transformations? For there are so many elements involved that we seem to have lost our way, and the question of what makes the world go round is still grinning at us, with a few more possible answers, such as

e) quarrels
f) passion
g) governesses
h) growing up.

We can rule out governesses for a start, because they mind other people's business; then, too, however fast the Red Queen made Alice run, they both remained in the same place. How about Passion? Now there is certainly more to that than gloves and kisses, as Carroll discovered when he wished to have a Passion-flower in the Garden of Live Flowers, that parody of Tennyson's 'Maud'. For a Passion-flower has nothing to do with losing your temper, or even the usual

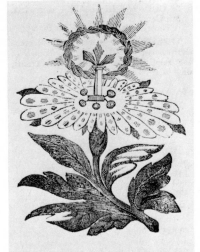

*From Hone's
Every Day Book
for June 8.*

𝔓𝔞𝔰𝔰𝔦𝔬𝔫 𝔉𝔩𝔬𝔴𝔢𝔯.

forms of romance, but symbolises the Crucifixion. When this was pointed out to him, he converted it to a Tiger-lily, though leaving the Red Queen with her crown of thorns. Why he did so can be inferred from an anecdote published by Collingwood (*Life and Letters*, p. 51), in which a friend asked Carroll if the final scene of *Looking-glass* was based on the triumphal conclusion of *Pilgrim's Progress*. 'He repudiated the idea, saying that he would consider such trespassing on holy ground as highly irreverent.' (Collingwood

81

noted the same trait in Carroll's father the Archdeacon: 'His reverence for sacred things was so great that he was never known to relate a story which included a jest upon words from the Bible.') That one can be a trespasser without meaning to be, however, is plain from the several meanings that *passion* has acquired; and the fact that he forgot its religious sense is interesting when you remember that he was a deacon, his father an archdeacon, and his great-grandfather a bishop. What he knew of the consequences of the Passion is therefore something we must now courteously investigate.

On April 12, 1857, he wrote in his diary:

> Lloyd preached the college sermon ... He mentioned one doctrinal point quite new to me: viz. that the Crucifixion without the Resurrection would only have atoned for past sins, and not for any which had not been committed.

When *Looking-glass* was published thirteen years later, the doctrine had undergone some change. For, as the White Queen said,

> '. . . there's the King's Messenger. He's in prison now, being punished: and the trial doesn't even begin till next Wednesday; and of course the crime comes last of all.'
> 'Suppose he never commits the crime?' said Alice.
> 'That would be all the better, wouldn't it?'

Soon after this the White Queen began to bleat and turned into a Sheep, no doubt as a result of trying to believe six impossible things before breakfast. But this of course is in *Looking-glass*, and she has a memory that works both ways. Before we tackle this poser, let us clear the air★ with a game of our own invention, that of rhyming Doublets together.

> Dip Pen into Ink,
> Drive Pig into Sty,
> Change Blue into Pink,
> Make Eel into Pie.
>
> Evolve Man from Ape,
> Make Hare into Soup,
> Change Cain into Abel,
> Prove Pity to be Good.

---

★ Gertrude Chataway can tell us how Carroll did so when on holiday: 'he would come on to his balcony, which joined ours, sniffing the sea-air with his head thrown back, and would walk right down to the beach with his chin in air, drinking in the fresh breezes as if he could never have enough.' (Collingwood, *Life and Letters*, p. 379.) With this in mind, it is worth remarking on the lack of any allusion in his writings to the sense of smell.

Cain and Abel are, of course, the first human rivals in the Bible, and after Abel's murder Cain was driven forth to be a vagabond, but with a mark on his forehead lest anyone finding him should kill him. Folklore transformed him into the Wandering Jew and the Man in the Moon, who should have no rest until the end of Time. Problem: does the Last Judgment find him innocent or guilty? And what is the punishment, if any?

There are several possible answers. Here are two, put into Alice's mouth:

> 'That's three faults, Kitty, and you've not been punished for any of them yet. You know I'm saving up all your punishments for Wednesday week – Suppose they had saved up all *my* punishments? . . . What *would* they do at the end of a year? I should be sent to prison, I suppose, when the day came. Or – let me see – suppose each punishment was to be going without a dinner: then, when the miserable day came, I should have to go without fifty dinners at once! Well, I shouldn't mind *that* much! I'd far rather go without them than eat them!'

That miserable day, which elsewhere is said to summon to unwelcome bed a melancholy maiden, led Carroll to consider a third possibility during the last year of his life in

## ETERNAL PUNISHMENT

The most common form of the difficulty, felt in regard to this doctrine, may be thus expressed: –

'I believe that God is perfectly good. Yet I seem compelled to believe that He will inflict Eternal Punishment on certain human beings in circumstances which would make it, according to my conscience, unjust, and therefore wrong.'

This difficulty, when stated in logical form, will be found to arise from the existence of *three* incompatible Propositions, each of which has, apparently, a strong claim for our assent. They are as follows: –

I.   God is perfectly good.
II.  To inflict Eternal Punishment on certain human beings, and in certain circumstances, would be wrong.
III. God is capable of acting thus.

One mode of escape from this difficulty is, no doubt, to let the whole subject alone. But . . .

But once you have started, Rule 12 comes into force and you must go on until you reach the end. However, we can afford to take a short cut that leads directly to the four possible solutions to this dilemma, which Carroll held would not violate the laws of logical

"He gave it to his father."  Ossian.

reasoning, however much they might those of sensibility. We can summarise them thus:

1) It is wrong for God to be right eternally, if that does wrong to others.
2) It is right for Him to be so.
3) The Bible is wrong to declare that 2) is correct.
4) The word *aion*, which the English Bible translates as 'eternally', really means 'of unknown duration'.

Carroll favoured the last solution, which would prove that Pity is Good. It also allows Cain to turn into Abel so that, if it is a quarrel that makes the world go round, the change should bring the world to a stop. However, *Looking-glass* shows that this does not occur, for to change Cain into Abel merely creates those two Abels called Tweedledum and Tweedledee. These twins, though each nominally one of the White Rooks, inhabit the same square of the chessboard – and what do they do there but raise Cain?

This situation was in fact adumbrated in the *Dynamics*, as

PROP. V. PR.

To continue a given series.

*Example*. A and B, who are respectively addicted to Fours and Fives, occupy the same set of rooms, which is always at Sixes and Sevens. Find the probable amount of reading done by A and B while the Eights are on.

It is thus evident that Pity has no place in the Last Judgment, because when Cain changes into Abel all that happens is that the series giving rise to their quarrel is continued in the same set of rooms. A quarrel is thus essential to make the world go round, especially – as we shall see – when it has to do with things at sixes and sevens. This deduction lets us adduce other rules for the Game:

Rule 16. *No final judgment can be passed on whether a series is ended or not.*

Rule 17. *If there is a difference between two players on which no final judgment is possible, the one who settles it to his own advantage by moving out of time is deemed to have lost the point.*

We are talking here, of course, of the Hatter, who was punished for a crime of a most unusual sort, the kind that may not even be committed. How can this be, unless the crime is indeed to murder the time that would lead to the event in question? For any other solution to the Riddle would put the cause of Original Sin in the future, and make the descendants of Adam his ancestors. It would also force the Resurrection to precede the Crucifixion, which is a totally unsound theological proposition. To escape from this heresy, we need

Rule 18. *To avoid being punished for a difference that is still in the future, change partners. The difference will then allow the present to appear constant.*

Carroll gave several demonstrations of the Rule. Here are three of them, the first being the performance of the Lobster Quadrille. You start with two lines,★ change lobsters, and retire in the same order. Then you throw the lobsters out to sea, swim after them, turn a somersault, change lobsters, and back to land. That's the first figure, at the end of which you discover that the whitings, who insist on joining the dance because they have a porpoise in mind, end with their tails stuck fast in their mouths. What is the figure they make? Answer: 0.

The second demonstration puts other figures to the dance: it is one of Carroll's Pillow Problems.

Put down any number of pounds not more than twelve, any number of shillings under twenty, and any number of pence

---

★To estimate the direction of such a line, we may consult PROP. III. PR. in the second chapter of the *Dynamics*:

*Example.* Prove that the definition of a line, according to Walton, coincides with that of Salmon, only that they begin at opposite ends.

George Salmon, 1819–1904, was a mathematician and divine, author of such works as *The Eternity of Future Punishment* (1864) and *Higher Plane Curves* (1852).

under twelve. Under the pounds put the number of pence, under the shillings put the number of shillings, and under the pence put the number of pounds.

Subtract.

Reverse the line again.

Add.

Answer, £12.18s.11d., *whatever* numbers may have been selected.★

The third is the story of *Wonderland*. We can put it into the form of the Pillow Problem thus:

Give a girl aged 7 a bottle labelled 'DRINK ME'. Then give

her a glass box containing a cake on which is written 'EAT ME'. Subtract the amount she grows from the amount she shrinks. Repeat, while reversing the effects of the liquid and the solid given.

Add the amount she shrinks to the amount she grows.

Answer, A mushroom that keeps a girl in Wonderland *whatever* size she becomes.

I take 7 to be the age of the girl because, though Alice was 10 years old when *Wonderland* was first told, Carroll wrote to her when she was 39 that he could scarcely picture her to himself as more than 7 years old. So, though the answer to the question,

---

★ We must correct Carroll here: the answer is only possible if the number of pounds is greater than the number of pence.

What makes the world go round? *should* be 'growing up', Rule 18 has come into force and changed all that. The result is that the real Alice has turned into Carroll's dream-child, and the duration of the dream cannot be known because it has murdered the time that turns a present reality into a future one. How has this happened? According to the White Queen, 'The rule is . . .'

Rule 19. 'jam to-morrow and jam yesterday, but never jam *to-day*.'

We can now identify Euclid's ever modern rival with some success: it is Time. For Time has no place in the eternal world of Euclidean geometry except in the 12th axiom, which differs from all the others in being disreputable – that is, it cannot be demonstrated. Euclid knew this well, but it took twenty-two centuries to prove so. Dodgson, however, thought that the axiom *could* be made reputable, and the approach he considered to be least unsatisfactory was to consider parallel lines as making 'equal angles with a certain transversal' (*A New Theory of Parallels*). His attitude to a temporal solution can be found in his *The Offer of the Clarendon Trustees* (1868) as requisite E:

A narrow strip of ground, railed off and carefully leveled, for investigating the properties of Asymptotes, and testing practically whether Parallel Lines meet or not: for this purpose it should reach, to use the expressive language of Euclid, 'ever so far'.

This last process, of 'continually producing the Lines', may require centuries or more: but such a period, though long in the life of an individual, is as nothing in the life of the University.

'Ever so far' refers to the problem of Unlimited Space which makes the 12th axiom disreputable. The logical nature of geometry forbade Dodgson to treat the subject as he had Eternity, and for 'Unlimited' substitute 'Indefinite'. His argument was that

*Both* conclusions – that Space has a limit, and that it has none – are *beyond* our Reason: but the former is also *against* our Reason, for we may fairly say 'When we have reached the limit, what then? What do we come to? There must be either Something, or Nothing. If Something, it is *full* Space, 'plenum'; if Nothing, it is *empty* Space, 'vacuum'. That there should be neither of these is absurd. Such an hypothesis is most intolerable.

(*A New Theory of Parallels*)

It is here that the difference between Carroll and Dodgson is most marked. For Dodgson could only geometrise on the flat, and had not read Riemann* (as he should have done), who showed that it is not beyond Reason to hold that Space can do without such limitations as 'full' and 'empty' as long as it is spherical. Carroll, however – as I claimed in the first chapter – was continually demonstrating à la Riemann that the unknown lying on the other side of Reason is, for Nonsense, nothing but the limit itself when viewed as the centre of a circle.

We are thus left with the conclusion that Carroll solved the problem of the 12th axiom, which Dodgson shelved. That Dodgson did not recognise the solution when Carroll saw it is due to many factors, some more interesting than others. At the heart of the difficulty, of course, is the fact that Dodgson was logical by the book and therefore reputable, while Carroll was logical by inspiration and, so to speak, disreputable. What this means can be found in an exception to the rule, namely *A Tangled Tale*. Carroll signed his name to this, though it mainly consists of Dodgsonian mathematical problems dressed up in amusing form: and in the Appendix, which treats the answers sent in by readers, he was sufficiently reputable to disbar all *accidental* solutions, and to describe those for which no working was given as 'beyond the reach of discussion'.

The tempting possibility therefore arises that, just as Riemannian geometry includes the Euclidean variety, so a Nonsense geometry could be formulated to include both. Although this is beyond the reach of the present enquiry, we can at least prepare for the task by giving the working for Nonsense and making it reputable. To this end we must again take up the general principle we have employed from the beginning, namely, that the geometer of Nonsense is included in the problem he faces. See him, then, producing a Line with his partner and reversing it in a looking-glass until the two of them reach the limit where there is Reason on both sides and Nonsense in the middle. The glass will then be found to contain an inspiring draught. But before we note the effects of this elixir, we must work out the prescription for the jam it is concealed in.

---

*'Riemann' sounds like a portmanteau composed of *Rhyme? and Reason?*, the title of a collection of verses published by Carroll in 1883. The name, of course, is that of the German mathematician (1826–66) who was the first to analyse all the assumptions of geometry, and to show that a surface can be both finite and unbounded. In *Mathematics and the Imagination* (1949), Kasner and Newman set out the Riemannian properties of the sphere in the following riddle:

A group of sportsmen, having pitched camp, set forth to go bear hunting. They walk 15 miles due south, then 15 miles due east, where they sight a bear. Bagging their game, they return to camp and find that altogether they have travelled 45 miles. What was the colour of the bear?

# Chapter VI

# Preserving Time

The distinction between reputable and disreputable axioms that Carroll used in *A New Theory of Parallels* is not altogether unlike that to be drawn between the acts that must stand in the last day before the judgment seat, and those that need not. Rule 19 shows that the matter in which the surd is expressed falls into both categories, for, the issue having been prejudged in such a way that no action is possible, it cannot be judged at all. This matter, nominally, is jam, for which we shall later adduce some Anglo-Saxon meanings. For the moment, however, we may follow the lead of Carroll's uncle, Hassard Dodgson, Master in Court of Common Pleas, who translated Jabberwocky into Latin –

> *Gaberbocchum.*
>
> *Hora aderat briligi. Nunc et Slythaeia Tova,*
> *Plurima gyrabant gymbolitare vabo . . .*

and do the same for Rule 19. The resultant pun is an old schoolboy favourite, and none the worse for that:

> *Jam quondam, et jam futurus, sed nunquam jam jam.*

When the Eternal Now is treated in this fashion we may expect the whirligig of Time to bring in some curious revenges. It had, in fact, already been so treated some twenty years before *Looking-glass* was written, and the heresy noted and duly combatted by Carroll's father the Archdeacon in a justificatory work called *The Controversies of Faith*. It concerned

> the peculiar view of Mr. Gorham, condemned by the Bishop of Exeter, [which] is, that no child is by Baptism regenerated, unless he receive it rightly; and that none can receive it rightly, unless he be previously regenerated.

The Archdeacon solved this poser by making use of such theological surds as can be found in the nature of the sacraments, in the innocence of children and the necessary presence of sponsors at the rite. Carroll was to do much the same in dealing with Rule 19, but in a way unorthodox enough for it to have had some unexpected results. Since the Rule is strangely bound up with the answer Carroll gave to the Riddle we must look at it in more detail and, as ever, by means

*Archdeacon Dodgson. Photo by C.L.D.*

of parallels. Let us therefore quote a further rule which, though the twentieth by our reckoning, is Carroll's Rule 42 – a fact which, though fortuitous, is (as we shall see) appropriate. It appears during the Trial scene in *Wonderland*, thus:

Rule 42. '*All persons more than a mile high to leave the court.*'

and is followed by this dialogue:

'Well, I shan't go, at any rate,' said Alice; 'besides, that's not a regular rule: you invented it just now.'

'It's the oldest rule in the book,' said the King.

'Then it ought to be Number One,' said Alice.

So it ought, and so we shall find it is. But we have another Rule 42 to deal with, which appears in the Preface to *The Hunting of the Snark*. There it is given as '*No one shall speak to the Man at the Helm*', complete with the Bellman's addition, '*and the Man at the Helm shall speak to no one*'. The figure 42 reappears in the *Snark* as the number of boxes the Baker brought with him, though they were all left behind on the beach when the ship sailed; and we may also find it as the unstated product of the seven coats and three pairs of boots he was wearing at the time. (If *added* together they will make up a Baker's dozen.)

The Baker said, quite clearly, that he was 40 years old when he embarked. What may be an obsessive interest in numbers leads one to ask why he was not 42. The answer, presumably, is that the journey – which is stated to have taken many months – lasted two years, no doubt because the ship so often sailed backwards. The number 40 also appears in connection with the pig that the Snark was 'defending' on the charge of leaving its sty. Found guilty, it was sentenced to transportation for life, 'and *then* to be fined forty pounds'. The similarity of its fate to that of the Baker encourages us to amend this sentence by a small transposition that does not affect the metre, and the addition of a surd, to 'and *then* be fined forty-two pounds'.★

---

★But 40 is a peculiar number itself. For instance, Chapter XVIII of *Sylvie and Bruno* is entitled 'Queer Street, Number Forty'. The address turns out to be that of the *right* house in the wrong *street*, reached after observations of perfectly isochronous movement, and delivered by one who, having shouted the number in stentorian tones, added 'And not *piano*, by any means!'

This does not entirely explain the queerness of forty and nor does a later passage, where the Professor is speaking: 'In giving birthday presents, my motto is – cheapness! I should think I save forty pounds a year by giving – oh what a twinge of pain!' (The twinge is immediately redefined as 'my old enemy', lumbago, but that is merely a cover for what he means.) But we can find an explanation in the Preface to *Sylvie and Bruno Concluded* where Carroll writes down the *theory* on which the story is constructed. 'It is an attempt to show what might *possibly* happen, supposing that Fairies really existed; and that they were sometimes visible to us, and we to them; and that they were sometimes able to assume human form: and supposing, also, that human beings might sometimes become conscious of what goes on in the Fairy-world – by actual transference of their immaterial essence, such as we meet with in "Esoteric Buddhism".' The switch from one world to the other, from waking to dreaming and back again, operates continuously throughout the book, and comes to a happy conclusion: wherefore we may say with the Master in *Sylvie and Bruno* (Chapter XIII), 'forty winks will do you no harm'.

If this be allowed, we already have six 42s. A seventh appears in the coincidence that Carroll was 42 when the last line of the *Snark* (which was the first in order of composition) came to him while taking a walk near Guildford in 1874. But what kind of an age is this? Already when he was 37 and writing 'Phantasmagoria' the haunted hero of that ghost story declared he was 42; and *Wonderland* was written when he was 30.

That gives a total of eight 42s, and we can find another two in the number of illustrations Tenniel drew for each of the *Alices*, though he increased the number in *Looking-glass* to 50 before publication. An eleventh can be found in 4207, the number of soldiers the White King sent to pick up the ruins of Humpty Dumpty, and a twelfth in Humpty Dumpty himself. For he originally was an egg in the Sheep's shop, the going price there being 'Fivepence farthing for one – twopence for two.'

'Then two are cheaper than one?' . . .
'Only you *must* eat them both, if you buy two.'

Granted that students at Christ Church complained that they had to order two eggs for breakfast on the chance of getting one that wasn't bad, why does a single one cost fivepence farthing? There is no stipulation that you should eat it, if you buy it: but once you *ate* it you would realise that the odds against it being a bad egg had been multiplied by your action to 1 in 42.

The rationale of 42 is to be found hidden at the beginning of *Wonderland* just after Alice has shrunk, grown, and shrunk again. She wonders, after these transformations, just who she is – '*that's* the great puzzle!' she says. Perhaps she has changed into another girl of her own age? This line leading nowhere, she tries to remember what she used to know, such as the Multiplication Table.

'Let me see: four times five is twelve, and four times six is thirteen, and four times seven is – oh dear! I shall never get to twenty at that rate!'

This is not the nonsense it appears to be, as Taylor (p. 47) has cunningly worked out. For if, instead of using the normal scale of 10 when you multiply $4 \times 5$, you use the scale of 18, this is the result:

1 2 3 4 5 6 7 8 9 (10 11 12 13 14 15 16 17) 10 11 12

which contains the requisite 20 digits for scale 10, and the 12 of scale 18. Similarly, $4 \times 6$ is 13 on scale 21:

1 2 3 4 5 6 7 8 9 (10 11 12 13 14 15 16 17 18 19 20) 10 11 12 13

which contains the requisite 24 digits.

Thus, each time you increase the multiplier by one, the product will also increase by one as long as you increase the scale by 3. This holds good until you reach 4 × 13, by which time scale 42 must be used:

1 2 3 4 5 6 7 8 9 (10 11 12 13 . . . 40 41) 10 11 12 . . . 19 20.

This contains the requisite 52 digits for scale 10, but the last figure is not really 20 at all. For just as the 12 given as the product of 4 × 5 is really 1–2, and the 13 of 4 × 6 is 1–3, so – logically – the 20 which is the product of 4 × 13 on scale 42 is 1–10. A little work will show that starting the series with 4 × 5 on scale 18 one can in fact never reach 20 at all, however far one goes.

The numerology involved when you arrive at 4 × 13 on scale 42 is curious enough to be noted. This is the moment in the system when one logic apparently contradicts another, so that they are at sixes and sevens. They are so quite literally, of course, because 6+7 is 13 and 6 × 7 is 42. Then, just as 4 is twice 2 so, if you wish to arrive at 20 on scale 42, you can only do so by doubling the multiplicand: 8 × 13 is 2 − 0, the equivalent of 104 on scale 10.

With this in mind, let us seek elsewhere for the number 4 (which, as a note in Chapter VIII will show, marks a surd) and its half.* As we have mentioned, the story entitled 'Novelty and Romancement' starts off on a Friday, the 4th of June, at half-past four p.m. Carroll began writing this story on January 21, 1856, when he was six days short of his 24th birthday – and 24 is, of course, 42 reversed. He must have met Alice for the first time later on in the year of 1856, and she would then have been 4 years old. She was born on Tuesday, May 4, 1852, while the boating trip on which her adventures underground were told took place on Friday, July 4, 1862. *Looking-glass* begins on the day before Guy Fawkes Day, which is therefore November 4; and Alice there tells Humpty Dumpty that she is 7 years and 6 months old. And then there is the chapter on Peter and Paul in Chapter XI of *Sylvie and Bruno*, which deals with Paul forcing a loan of £50 on Peter on April 1 to be repaid by noon, the 4th of May – a loan which is never actually made, though Peter is legally forced to pay it back.

As for half-past four, this is just after *brillig*, the time you start broiling things for dinner, and the very hour that the Tweedles started to fight, having agreed to go on till six and then have supper.

---

* That 4 and 2 are questionable numbers may be seen by consulting the Code (p. 52 above), where 4 can be q and 2, w; these letters being the initials for the interrogative in Latin and English.

Six $(4+2)$ was the hour during which the Hatter was always having tea,★ this being the moment when he murdered time at the Queen of Hearts' concert. The murder also put his watch out by two days. This matter has been studied by Professor L. J. Russell (Taylor, p. 57), who went to the trouble of consulting an almanac: and he discovered that on May 4, 1862, the solar and lunar calendars were exactly two days out of coincidence. Whether Carroll knew this or not, the missing 2 is again found in the March Hare's attendance at the Mad Tea-party in May, two months out of his season; while *Wonderland* was told two months to the day after Alice's birthday.

It thus seems possible that for 42 one can read half-past four and vice versa, for both these numbers are connected with some curious stoppages and act as surds in the computation of Time. $4\frac{1}{2}$ also figures as money, first in the *original* version of the White Knight's Song, where after the Aged Aged Man tells how he made Rowland's Macassar Oil by setting water on fire, he says:

> 'But fourpence-halfpenny is all
> They give me for my toil.'

Later we have the Professor in *Sylvie and Bruno* giving Sylvie a second-hand pincushion, which he bought for $4\frac{1}{2}$d.

Let us now repeat the two Rules 42:

a) *'All persons more than a mile high shall leave the court.'*
b) *'No one shall speak to the Man at the Helm, and the Man at the Helm shall speak to no one.'*

That these two rules face in opposite directions from the same point can be seen in *Looking-glass* which, by a nice coincidence, was published when Alice had reached the still possible age of 19. She was already growing when Rule 42a was invented: but when Humpty Dumpty said, 'If you'd asked *my* advice, I'd have said "Leave off at seven"', she replied indignantly, 'I never ask advice about growing.' (There's Rule 42b for you, broken twice over on account of Rule 42a.) By this she meant that one can't help growing older. Humpty Dumpty, however, replied with Rule 42 transformed into the oldest one in the book:

---

★ In 1874, Carroll wrote: '"Five o'clock tea" is a phrase that our "rude forefathers" even of the last generation, would hardly have understood, so completely is it a thing of today; and yet, so rapid is the March of Mind, it has already risen into a national institution, and rivals, in its universal application to all ranks and ages, and as a specific "for all the ills that flesh is heir to", the glorious Magna Charta.' ('The Blank Cheque'.)

Rule 1. *You may come and go simultaneously, as long as there are two of you.*

In Humpty Dumpty's mouth, this became

Rule 1a. '*One* can't, perhaps, but *two* can.'

Two *must*, indeed, as a look at the end part of Carroll's *Curiosa Mathematica* will show. This is a collection of 72 Pillow Problems, ten of which have to do with black and white counters, or in one case red and white ones, put into one, two or three bags, and variously mixed: the problem being to know what chance there is of drawing out a white counter. We can discover what kind of a meaning this had for Carroll from his diaries. For instance, on April 25, 1856, he wrote:

> Went over with Southey in the afternoon to the Deanery, to try and take a photograph of the Cathedral: both attempts proved failures. The three little girls were in the garden most of the time, and we became excellent friends: we tried to group them in the foreground of the picture, but they were not patient sitters. I mark this day with a white stone.

He marked other happy occasions with a white stone (rather than a red letter), and his Pillow Problems parallel the chancy occurrence of these – with one exception, which throws some light on the nature of Rule 1a. It is not only the last in the book, but the only one which he alludes to in his Introduction, thus:

> If any of my readers should feel inclined to reproach me with having worked too uniformly in the region of Commonplace, and with never having ventured out of this beaten track, I can proudly point to my one Problem in 'Transcendental Probabilities' – a subject in which, I believe, *very* little has yet been done by even the most enterprising of mathematical explorers. To the casual reader it may seem abnormal and even paradoxical; but I would have such a reader ask himself, candidly, the question 'Is not Life itself a Paradox?'

The reader may like to note the number of Ps in this passage, the letter on which he most usually stuttered. The Problem itself, which is dated September 8, 1887, runs as follows:

> A bag contains two counters, as to which nothing is known except that each is either black or white. Ascertain their colours without taking them out of the bag.

The answer – arrived at by putting another white stone into the bag, and using some disreputable mathematical tricks – is: One is black, and the other white. How else could there be any problem?

But what kind of problem is it? We have had some view of its enormity, in Carroll's essay on Eternal Punishment: but even there he has used his sleight-of-hand to such effect that Cain can become Abel, as long as Abel becomes Cain. We have thus come back to our circular argument, with the added insight that two are enough to start it off, as long as there is a difference between them – a difference that is felt most when it concerns love, or passion, or age. In order to un-snark this argument we may return to the question posed after Rule 9 was brought in: on what is a circular argument supported?

On the bowsprit? the rudder? the ship?
On the sea?
On the Boojum?

Let us try the sea, in honour of the nursery rhyme 'If all the world were paper, And all the sea were ink ...' We are at Whitby, in 1854, when Carroll was 22; he then wrote a story called 'Wilhelm von Schmitz'. The real name of this hero was William Smith, of Yorkshire, but he took to the German form when he found it embarrassing to answer questions about his ancestry.* He was, you see, a poet.

> For a while he gazed down dreaming upon the expanse of Ocean, then, struck by a sudden thought, he opened a small pocket book, and proceeded to correct and complete his last poem. Slowly to himself he muttered the words 'death – saith – breath', impatiently tapping the ground with his foot. 'Ah, that'll do,' he said at last, with an air of relief: 'breath'.

---

*Carroll himself may have been so embarrassed, but for quite different reasons. Green (*Diaries*, p. 2) has traced the roots of the Dodgson family tree back to a Sir Charles Hoghton, who descended by Adam de Hoghton from Matilda, the illegitimate daughter of William the Conqueror:

> In this descent Sir Richard de Hoghton ... who died in 1340, married Sybell, daughter of Sir William de Lea, directly descended from Yvo de Talbois, ... who ... married Lucia the sister of the Earls Edwin and Morcar and granddaughter of Leofric the Great, Earl of Mercia (died 1057) by his wife Lady Godiva. It is improbable that Lewis Carroll knew of this relationship, or else the fortunes of Edwin and Morcar (as described by Havilland Chepmell in his *Short Course of History*, 1862, pp. 143–4) might not have been dismissed by the Mouse in *Wonderland* as 'the driest thing I know'! He may, however, have known that among his ancestors was Sir Richard Hoghton, the first baronet, at whose table in 1611 King James the First conferred the order of knighthood upon a 'loin' of beef – before proceeding to cut the first sirloin in defiance of all etiquette!

I take leave to doubt Carroll's ignorance of his descent from Edwin and

'His barque had perished in the storm,
    Whirled by its fiery breath
On sunken rocks, his stalwart form,
    Was doomed to watery death.

'That last line's good,' he continued exultingly, 'and on Coleridge's principle of alliteration too – W.D., W.D. – was doomed to watery death.'

'Take care,' growled a deep voice in his ear, 'what you say will be used in evidence against you . . .'

We shall, of course, set this evidence down later. For we have begun, quite wrongly, in the middle of the story. The beginning has seen the Poet conversing with his friend, the Prose-writer Muggins. He then ignored a warning to 'tak whether o' the two roads thou likes, but thou ca'n't stop in't middle!' and fell into a canal when the drawbridge he was walking on opened to let a barge through. Dripping wet, he made his way to an inn where he overheard a Waiter mention the name of his inamorata, a certain Sukie. What the Waiter *said* was that he hoped 'to hacquire her Hart', but what he meant was her Art, of serving at table. (He later de-aspirated this word, saying 'when the 'art of man is hopressed with care'.) The Poet started up in indignation, offered to punch the Waiter and then, on finding out his mistake, made reparation by standing him a glass of punch. It was, if Dr Johnson will allow it, a seaside Pun-ch and Sukie show; and the Waiter, being a forgiving sort, then proposed a toast: ' "I'll give you – Woman! She doubles our sorrows, and 'alves our joy." The Poet drained the glass, not caring to correct

---

Morcar, though on admittedly shaky grounds. For a start, his quotation from Chepmell breaks off just before William's barons, supported by Edwin and Morcar, are said to have risen against him in a Revolution led by Hereward the Wake. As we shall see, the punishment that goes with a Revolution is to have one's head cut off, the obvious victim being Charles I. But the name William crops up so often in Carroll, beautifully decapitated in the cry of 'Rilchiam!' that we may suspect it to be a disguise for Charles Dodgson – the reason being, as Alice said of the Mouse, that he had come over with William the Conqueror. Interestingly enough, though the Red Queen advised Alice to 'Speak in French, when you ca'n't think of the English for a thing', Carroll himself only set himself to learn French in 1881. Finally, Carroll's youngest brother was christened Edwin – a nice coincidence but not one, of course, that *proves* anything.

A doubt of a different kind is raised by what Green has to say about Sir Richard Hoghton: it may be that the B we have assigned to the Bishop should more fittingly be given to the first Baronet, though this need not overthrow our argument.

his companion's mistake.' The punch finally hit the Waiter so hard that, after trying to repeat this toast, he doubled himself up and vanished under the table.

The Poet then made his way to the cliffs, where he composed the verse we cited at the start. Enter, then, the Prose-writer, with the Law. Where is the Waiter? 'Dr — ' says the Poet, much confused. Drowned? Luckily the Waiter appears on the scene and sets all to rights; and the Prose-writer repents of his evil suspicions by presenting the Poet and his bride with a License to sell to all, Spirits, Porter, Snuff and Ale, in an Inn of his own. (This is the kidney punch, for in Carroll's poem 'Atalanta in Camden Town' 'the question is "License or Banns?" though undoubtedly Banns are the cheapest'. Moreover, if the Poet had been ordained – which he was seven years later, as a deacon – the Prose-writer should have given him a Living rather than a License.)★

---

★The following syllogism from Carroll's *Symbolic Logic* affords interesting evidence as to the connection between the poet, the law, and what waiters often serve their customers:

1. All the policemen on this beat sup with our cook.
2. No man with long hair can fail to be a poet.
3. Amos Judd has never been in prison.
4. Our cook's 'cousins' all love cold mutton.
5. None but policemen on this beat are poets.
6. None but her 'cousins' ever sup with our cook.
7. Men with short hair have all been in prison.

The conclusion? 'Amos Judd loves cold mutton.' And the application? 'Your hair wants cutting,' said the Hatter; who cannot have been a poet or he would not have gone to prison. (But how it was that Tenniel drew him with long hair must be left for the moment.)

Here now is the evidence, with items from other cases to refresh the memory:

| 1 | 2 | 5 | 6 | 0 |
|---|---|---|---|---|
| b | d | l | s | r |
| c | w | v | | |
| | White | | | Rabbit |
| Carpenter | Walrus | | | |
| Baronet | | | | |
| Conqueror | William | | | Richard |
| Bishop | D.D. | | | Right |
| | | | | Reverend |
| | Dean | Venerable | | |
| | Deacon | | | Reverend |
| Charles | Dodgson | Lutwidge | | |
| Carroll | | Lewis | | |
| Bellman *et al.* | | | | |
| Boojum | | | Snark | |
| Cheshire Cat | | Vanishing | | |
| bow | | | sprit | rudder |
| bride-cake | | | | |
| coats | | | shoes | |
| | | | | raving mad |
| | wine | | | no room |
| | | | | remarks |
| | | very | | rude |
| | eyes wide | | | |
| | why is | | | |
| | writing-desk | | | raven |
| | Watch | | | riddles |
| | wrong | | | |
| | Whitby | | sea | |
| | William | | Smith | |
| | drawbridge | | | |
| companion | Waiter | | Sukie | rival |
| | drunk | | | |
| breath | death | | saith | |
| barque | whirled | | sunken | rocks |
| | | | stalwart | |
| Coleridge | was | | | |
| | doomed | | | |
| | watery | | | |
| | death | | | |
| | drowned | | | |
| | Woman! | | | |

The reader will recognise the form of this set-up as originating in Carroll's number code. Much of it has no particular application, though it shows how a permutational table could be drawn up for use in playing the game of Anglo-Saxon Attitudes. If some of it now adds up to anything, this can only be coincidence, whatever we may like to mean by the word. But, as the Archbishop said in his Sermon, 'Nothing is prejudged, and nothing is condemned, but upon such proof, as the nature of the thing requires, the testimony of others'; and having testimony of a kind, let us without prejudice translate, for instance, the Waiter's Toast into numbers.

'Woman! She doubles our sorrows, and 'alves our joy!'

The result, though not gained by a strict application of Carroll's rules, is something impossible to believe before breakfast. For, by his number code, w stands for 2, s for 6 and j for 3. If we double s by w, the product is 12 sorrows; if we halve j, we get one and a half joys. The mistake, in spite of the Poet's *laissez-faire*, must be corrected. Doubled joys then are 6, and halved sorrows, 3; and since 6 is twice 3, the amended toast to Woman! proves indeed to be the right one.★

We can also take advantage of this evidence, though without its numerological consequences, by considering the Was Drowned of W.D. in connection with the Waiter's (presumed) rivalry. For this we must move to *Bruno's Revenge*, published in 1867, three years after *Wonderland*. Bruno is the brownie or elf that 'Alice's Hour in Elfland' was waiting for, and so is Sylvie – though she is, nominally, a sylph. Elves, said Carroll, 'are something of the nature of will-o'-the-wisps', which adds a useful piece of information to our knowledge of Boojums. However, it is more proper to say that they are angels, and Bruno is unique in being the only boy that Carroll ever wrote about without wanting to turn him into a pig. Throughout the tale he calls himself 'B'uno', being a regular ellipser of r-s

---

★The oddity of the procedure which leads to the precision of this result is not a matter for argument. The result, however, is: and we can perhaps throw some light on it and other such coincidental truths by quoting Watkins H. Williams, who was one of Carroll's students. Here is his account of all that passed between them during his first tutorial in the early 1860s: 'He took me last, and, glancing at a problem of Euclid which I had written out, he placed his finger on an omission. "I deny your right to assert that." I supplied what was wanting. "Why did you not say so before? What is a corollary?" Silence. "Do you ever play billiards?" "Sometimes." "If you attempted a cannon, missed and holed your own and the red ball, what would you call it?" "A fluke." "Exactly. A corollary is a fluke in Euclid. Good morning."' (Quoted in Green, *Diaries*, p. 67.) I may add that the slang for a fluke in billiards was then 'a regular Crow'.

rather than a lisper of them, except when it comes to two words. Here he is talking about Sylvie, while busily uprooting her garden:

'The nasty c'oss thing – wouldn't let me go and play this morning, though I wanted to ever so much – said I must finish my lessons first – lessons, indeed! – I'll vex her though!'

'Oh, Bruno, you shouldn't do that,' I cried. 'Don't you know that's revenge? And revenge is a wicked, cruel, dangerous thing!'

'River-edge?' said Bruno. 'What a funny word! I suppose you call it c'ooel and dangerous because if you went too far and tumbled, you'd get d'owned.'

| B'uno | wicked | lessons | Sylvie | revenge |
|-------|--------|---------|--------|---------|
| cruel | dangerous | vex | | |
| | d'owned | | | river-edge |

He later pronounces 'revenge' without elision, and the story ends with Sylvie trying vainly to get him to repeat his new word with its proper pronunciation. So, having asked a question about when is a w not sounded, we must do the same for the r, but in reverse:

'When is an r sounded, being otherwise elided?'
The answer must be, 'When you drown something in revenge for lessons, indeed.'

We may pass quickly over Carroll's well-known hatred of the ordinary kind of lessons, which he was always deriding and parodying, and his own failure to inspire his undergraduate students: though we may note that he enjoyed giving lessons very much, as long as his pupils were loving, young, and saw the point of the Nonsense he wrapped his logic in. It must be noted, however, that the water in which revenge is drowned comes from tears; this leads us back to the beginning of *Wonderland*, when Alice met the Mouse swimming in her pool of tears. Also, and to more purpose, to the fact that *river-edge* is, etymologically, the same as *rival*.

We dealt with rivals – or couples, which come to the same thing – in our last chapter, and announced that this one would give the prescription for the jam in which the Elixir of Nonsense is made. We have, of course, been doing so from the beginning, for we remarked then that any arguments to do with the Riddle could, if necessary, be produced to infinity, and that the questions they deal with would be found, on the whole, to lie in parallel. Here, then, jammed between parallel banks, is Time, like an ever-rolling stream. The hour is half-past four on the fourth, when the oldest and newest Rules in the book are at sixes and sevens and the Tweedle brothers have started to fight. The watchword is 'brillig', but so rapid is the March of Mind that Tea-Time has become a national institution and rivals, as a specific 'for all the ills that flesh is heir to', the glorious Magna Charta. But tea is not the elixir we are looking for.

Chapter VII

# The black draught

'I shall never forget one afternoon when we had been walking in Christ Church meadows,' wrote Isa Bowman. 'We were going quietly along by the side of the "Cher", when he began to explain to me that the tiny stream was a tributary, "a baby river" as he put it, of the big Thames. He talked for some minutes, explaining how rivers came down from hills and flowed eventually into the sea, when he suddenly met a brother Don at a turning in the Avenue.' (*The Story of Lewis Carroll*, p. 13.)

That sounds like the beginning of an Adventure: but the meeting only made him stutter, as did the moment when the stream in a girl's life met the river, as he put it, and she put up her hair. That moment made all the difference, and he would usually no longer talk to her. It was better when he and the baby river were in a boat together on the big Thames, with a fellow Don rowing stroke and him in the bows telling stories:

> And ever, as the story drained
>     The wells of fancy dry,
> And faintly strove that weary one
>     To put the subject by,
> 'The rest next time' – 'It *is* next time!'
>     The happy voices cry.

The happy voices must have said other things too, such as 'There's no such thing!' when the Dormouse specified the well of fancy as a treacle-well – for there was a treacle-well near Binsey,★ as Carroll

---

★ The well is still there, a few yards from the door of St Margaret's church. Pinned to the inner door is the following notice:

S. FRIDESWIDE – A Saxon Princess in her own right founded a nunnery where the cathedral now stands. Her shrine is there for all to see. Due to the attention of ALFGAR, a courtier, Frideswide with her Ladies resorted to a cell at Thornbury & ALFGAR pressed his suit to which the Saint objected. He continuing his amours was struck by a lightning flash. The Saint in her piety prayed to S. Margaret of ANTIOCH who on appearance instructed Frideswide to strike the ground with her staff. On doing so water gushed out of the soil & bathing the Prince's eyes his sight was restored & clearly seeing the folly of his ways returned to Oxford a happier and wiser man. (*continued next page*)

must then have delighted in telling them when they rowed past it on the way to Godstow. Its water was used for healing, as the derivation of *treacle* from *theriac*, an antidote against snake poison, implies. He was well into that kind of well,★ as he one day confessed to a certain Mr Girdlestone: 'He said that in the company of very little children his brain enjoyed a rest which was startlingly recuperative. If he had been working too hard or had tired his brain in any way, to play with children was like an actual material tonic to his whole system. I understood him to say that the effect was almost physical!' (Quoted by Isa Bowman, p. 59.)

Let us put this into the language of Mr Gorham. 'No-one is by theriac recuperated, unless he receive it rightly; and none can receive it rightly, unless he be previously recuperated.' How can anyone then be recuperated? The answer must be, One can't, perhaps, but two can. To show the mutuality involved in taking a theriac, we shall quote this birthday letter written to Gertrude Chataway in 1875 (quoted in Green, *Diaries*, p. 387):

'Boohoo! here's Mr. Dodgson's drunk all my health, and I haven't any left!' And how it will puzzle Dr. Maund when he is sent for to see you! 'My dear Madam, I'm very sorry to say your little girl has got *no health at all*! I never saw such a thing in my life!' 'Oh, I can easily explain it!' your mother will say. 'You see she would go and make friends with a strange gentleman, and yesterday he drank her health!' 'Well, Mrs. Chataway, the only way to cure her is to wait until his next birthday, and then for *her* to drink *his* health!' And then we shall have changed healths. I wonder how you'll like mine? Oh Gertrude, I wish you would not talk such nonsense!

Whatever then happens to today's health, this transposition of tomorrow's into yesterday's allows the future to be read backwards into the past. The doubly literal proof of this is to be found in another letter, which Carroll wrote to Nelly Bowman in 1891 (quoted by Isa Bowman, p. 93):

C.L.D., Uncle loving your! Instead grandson his to it give to had you that so, years 80 or 70 for it forgot you that was it pity a what and: him of fond so were you wonder don't I and, gentleman old nice very a was he. For it made you that *him* been have

---

The reader may like to know that the cathedral is part of Christ Church, and that ALFGAR is Anglo-Saxon for *Elf-spear*.

★And indeed had been for a long time: according to Collingwood, the village of Croft where he spent most of his youth was renowned for baths and medicinal waters.

The Scanty Meal.
'The picture is intended, as our readers will perceive, to illustrate the evils of homeopathy★. This idea is well carried out through the whole picture.'
★ The science of taking medicine in infinitely small doses.

*must* it see you so: *grandfather* my was, *then* alive was that, 'Dodgson Uncle' only the. Born was *I* before long was that, see you, then But. 'Dodgson Uncle for pretty thing some make I'll now', it began you when, yourself to said you that, me telling her without, knew I course of and: ago years many great a it made had you said she. Me told Isa what from was it? For meant was it who out made I how know you do! Lasted has it well how and. Grandfather my for made had you Antimacassar pretty that me give to you of nice so was it, Nelly dear my.

But theriac, the agent of this mutuality, itself works in two directions. For *theriac* only came to mean 'medicine' because it originally meant 'snake-venom', the medicine being nothing less than a homeopathic dose of more snake-venom to cure the original poison. *Venom*, however, comes from the opposite direction, from *venenum*, a love philtre straight from Venus herself; just as *poison* comes from '(love-) potion'. To show the two movements involved we can express this simply as a proportion: Love turns to poison as poison turns to antidote. We can find this conclusion in a Carrollian piece of 1888, addressed to an American girls' school. The girls had asked permission to call their school magazine 'Jabberwocky', but soon printed something that offended Carroll's taste. He therefore sent them a 'Black Draught of serious remonstrance' and, on getting an apology, sent them in return a poem which fits our argument even to the title: 'A Lesson in Latin.' In the poem he first translates 'amare' as 'to love', and then as 'Bitter one!' ending with the respectable oxymoron that Love is Bitter-Sweet. But he also added a postscript, which makes one suspect that he not only wished to enjoy the double motion of a theriac, but to reverse the direction in which the proportion is made – 'Surely we can patiently swallow many "Black Draughts", if we are to be rewarded with so sweet a lump of sugar?' For the reward brings us back to the beginning again, the sugar of love having been the original villain of the piece. Anyone following the prescription is thus liable to be transformed into his past, and to require a daily dose of theriac to keep him there; what is more, it will still be jam yesterday and jam tomorrow when he gets there, and only black draughts today.

We must prove this assertion. What, for instance, is a black draught? Why, an infusion of senna compounded with sulphate of magnesia and extract of liquorice: formerly much used as a purgative, to compose internal dissensions. Nothing could have been more fittingly administered to Tweedledum and Tweedledee:

> *Just then flew down a monstrous crow,*
> *As black as a tar-barrel!*
> *Which frightened both the heroes so,*
> *They quite forgot their quarrel.*

In another form it was, of course, the principal agent by which the Head of the raven turned into the Tale of the writing-desk, when Alice asked Carroll to write down the story he had told her, her two sisters and his friend Duckworth that famous afternoon on the river. For ink is the black draught *par excellence* – did not Alice think of using a bottle of it to revive the White King at the beginning of *Looking-glass*, when he was feeling faint? And when she was Queened at the end, how else did all the creatures toast her but by singing in chorus:

> *Then fill up the glasses with treacle and ink,*
> *Or anything else that is pleasant to drink.*

We began by viewing the Riddle as a retort: now, obviously, it is time to see it as an inquiry. We do but follow Carroll in this, since the first word of his Answer is 'Enquiries' (see p. 21), which provides good grounds for us to agree with Carroll that the Answer is only fairly appropriate (as long, i.e., as it casts a spell on you). 'Because it is an inquiry' is in itself not a bad answer to the Riddle. You may gauge its aptness by taking a sheet from a quire of paper, laying it flat on the desk so that the wire-lines are perpendicular to the water-lines, and then turn BLACK into WHITE by dipping your pen (which is the name for a female swan) into the ink-well. Then wire into what you have to say ('wire into' – eat ravenously, work with vigour). Do this alliteratively, according to the rules of Nonsense by which one sound knocks another through the croquet hoops, until your opponent's ball is wired. That means to be placed just where it is hampered by a hoop. However, because a Nonsense player must assume the character of his opponent, he himself is the one to get out of the difficulty he has so ingeniously prepared. Sometimes this is not that easy, as Carroll remarked in a letter to Marion Richards (October 1881):

> Sometimes I get *that* confused I hardly know which is me and which is the ink-stand ... when it comes to putting bread-and-butter and orange-marmalade into the *ink-stand*: and then dipping pens into *oneself*, and filling *oneself* up with ink, you know, is horrid!

He would then have turned himself into a black-jack, namely a large jug (or, we might say, a juggins) for holding strong drink (and perhaps at other times used to jug a hare in).

All this may seem to be a laborious joke at Carroll's expense. But consider the fact that between 1870 and 1891 he always used violet ink and not black ('Dreadfully ugly, I used to think it,' wrote Isa Bowman). What shall we make of this? That nothing is merely black and white in Carroll? Or that he affected the purple, especially when he could parody the passages it coloured? Both reasons are helpful in coping with his rather flat take-off of Tennyson's 'Maud' ('Come into the garden, Maud, for the black bat, night, has flown ...') when Alice enters the Garden of Live Flowers. One of the flowers is the Violet, who declares it has never seen anyone who looked stupider than Alice. This earned it a well-merited rebuke from the Tiger-lily:

> 'Hold *your* tongue! ... As if *you* ever saw anybody! You keep your head under the leaves, and snore away there, till you know no more what's going on in the world, than if you were a bud!'

But the Tiger-lily, we remember, was originally a Passion-flower, and we know that Carroll shrank from two of the meanings of passion, regarding it principally as a synonym for bad temper. It seems to have been much the same with his use of violet ink, which stands in the same relation to black as a writing-desk to a raven.

But how about the black draught as a medicine against bad temper? If it is a theriac, it must itself have come *from* bad temper, or at least from its loss. This seems not unlikely where the Crow is concerned – which, as Alice remarked, flaps its wings so that it makes quite a hurricane in the woods. This clears the air, and cuts a quarrel down to its proper size. The same effect can be brought about by a fan. This can be seen during that parallel to the Trial scene, Alice's examination for the Queenship: the Red and White Queens have become quite quarrelsome with Alice, and when she becomes feverish they fan her head with leaves to cool her off. It can also be seen in the habit of the King's Messenger, who must have been a self-cooling quarrel or his Anglo-Saxon Attitudes would not have to end by him spreading his great hands like a fan on either side.

But this is only the half of it for, as we have intimated, a draught stops a quarrel from growing. Now, in fact, is the moment to complete our third demonstration of Rule 18, from which we omitted the middle term to simplify matters. For Alice must be made to shrink after she has eaten the little cake that makes her grow, and before she drinks from the bottle on the White Rabbit's table near the looking-glass, that also makes her grow: and this is done by making her pick up the White Rabbit's fan, which she uses to cool herself.★

Our argument is in danger of becoming windy, so we must ask ourselves what makes children grow in the first place. Carroll knew the answer to that one, as may be seen from the fact that he never allowed Isa Bowman to eat more than one rock cake when she was staying with him, and in the warning he sent to the mother of another young girl: 'Please be careful, because she eats a good deal too much.' As for Alice, she goes through her adventures with nothing to eat in *Wonderland* except for magical food and a slice

---

★In 'Alice's Adventures Underground' it is not the Rabbit's fan that Alice picks up, but his nosegay, which she smells. Had she been able to fan herself with it also, Carroll would have had no reason to make the change, for a nosegay and a fan both have the same general shape and, what is more, both can be made to *shut up*: though the effect is less noticeable in a nosegay with its individual flowers than in a fan. In any case, Alice only notices that the fan makes her shrink when she sees that somehow she has put on one of the Rabbit's gloves.

of bread and butter at the Tea-party, while in *Looking-glass* there is no cake left for her after she has handed it round to the Lion and the Unicorn, and she is forbidden to cut the leg of mutton after having

been introduced to it. It was only because she insisted on cutting the Pudding in order to eat it that her coronation feast came to its sudden and surprising end, with the White Queen screaming 'Something's going to happen!' And happen it did: Alice grew from a $7\frac{1}{2}$-year-old girl to a well-proportioned young woman of 19 in a flash, and woke up.

Having seen the effects of a theriac within, let us revert to the Crow and look for its effects on the tempest outside. The theriac, we must remember, is a logical piece of madness that comes over a man between March and July – the prescription obviously runs, 'A hare of the dog that bit him.' It is administered to girls when they become lumpish and bad-tempered, which sometimes happens when they have had a great deal too much food for thought: but it can also come as a love-potion, in the form of a fairy-tale.

> Child of the pure unclouded brow
> And dreaming eyes of wonder!
> Though time be fleet, and I and thou
> Are half a life asunder,
> Thy loving smile will surely hail
> The love-gift of a fairy-tale . . .

Come, hearken then, ere voice of dread,
   With bitter tidings laden,
Shall summon to unwelcome bed
   A melancholy maiden!
We are but older children, dear,
Who fret to find our bedtime near.

Without, the frost, the blinding snow,
   The storm-wind's moody madness –
Within, the firelight's ruddy glow
   And childhood's nest of gladness.
The magic words shall hold thee fast:
Thou shalt not heed the raving blast.
         (Verses from the introductory poem to *Looking-glass*)

Our inky theriac is proving to be a mixture of time, temper and tempest, which is etymologically proper since all three words are derived from the same root. It is also good Nonsense, and tells us the rule for being glad while living in a wood,★ which the White Queen could never remember. We must start with the raven, and transform its appearance and its voice simultaneously. Its blackness then separates out into the white of winter storms on the other side of the window, and the red glow of the firelight on this side; and its voice is transformed from a raving blast into magic words, which may be read after they have been heard.

The magic words shall hold thee fast ... What does go fast? Time, for a start: the White King will tell us that a minute goes by so fearfully quick that you might as well catch a Bandersnatch. But to go quick is not the same as to fast, or to be fast. To get the meaning of this last phrase we need to consult the White Knight, the Pudding inventor, who will tell us that he once fell into his own helmet and that the other White Knight then came and put it on, thinking it was his own. He took it off again after our Knight had kicked him on the head, 'but it took hours and hours to get me out. I was as fast – as fast as lightning, you know.'

How about lightning, then? Half a page after Alice has had her head cooled, she and the Queens have another little contretemps, after which the White Queen says, 'Don't let us quarrel', and asks, 'What is the cause of lightning?'

'The cause of lightning,' said Alice very decidedly, for she felt

---

★ ' "You might make a joke on *that*," said the little voice close to her ear: "something about 'you *would* if you could', you know."

(*Looking-glass*, Chapter III.)

*Photo of C. L. Dodgson's study at Christ Church, by C.L.D.*

quite certain about this, 'is the thunder – no no!' she hastily corrected herself. 'I meant the other way.'

'It's too late to correct it,' said the Red Queen: 'when you've once said a thing, that fixes it, and you must take the consequences.'

Let us then take the consequences. One of them is that lightning is fixed, just as the White Knight said it was. If the reader finds this conclusion too abrupt, he may continue to read from where our quotation breaks off, and will then find that there had been *such* a thunderstorm during one of the last set of Tuesdays.★ For in *Looking-glass* days come two or three at a time, and in winter as many as five together – because five nights are warmer than one. Are they not, by the same rule, five times as cold?

---

★'Tuesday, April 10 1877. Spent the day in London. It was (like so many Tuesdays in my life) a very enjoyable day.' So runs an entry in Carroll's diaries. More precisely, we have seen that *Looking-glass* is written as though it were six months after Alice's birthday adventures in *Wonderland*: and in 1862, November 4 fell on a Tuesday.

'Just so!' cried the Red Queen. 'Five times as warm, *and* five times as cold – just as I'm five times as rich as you are, *and* five times as clever!'

Alice sighed and gave it up. 'It's exactly like a riddle with no answer!' she thought.

That fits, for the w- of *warm* gives place to the r- of *rich*, like the change we found in the Riddle itself. And if there is no raven involved, at least there is the Crow, for the White Queen immediately follows on by saying, 'Humpty Dumpty saw it too', which seems to apply to this second riddle but refers back to the thunder, the storm or, what amounts to the same thing, a hippopotamus.

SIR J REYNOLDS PAINTER.                    *THE AGE OF INNOCENCE.*                    F JOUBERT ENGRAVER.
from the picture in the Vernon Gallery.

Humpty Dumpty said he *would* come in, the White Queen continued – out of the cold, we must deduce, to show the effect of a corkscrew on those who are egg-bound. We must now suspect that lightning is not forked, or sheet, but spiral – that Alice indeed got her answer the wrong way round. Surely, thunder is bolted as fast as a cork, and needs a corkscrew to make it pop. But none of this advances our argument. We must return to the White Queen, who declared that she was so frightened during her last thunderstorm that she couldn't remember her own name. There are many incidents scattered throughout the *Alices*, and in *The Hunting of the Snark*, that warn against this fatality, often alternating with injunctions not to lose one's temper. Let us then be Carrollian, and take the Gnat with its bad jokes as a contrary example. It remarked how convenient it would be if one managed to go home without a name, for if the governess wanted to call you to your lessons she would have to leave off because there wouldn't be any name to call. Alice replied that that wouldn't do, for the governess would call her 'Miss!' – though the Gnat made the rejoinder that she could then miss her lessons.

But even this won't do, for if a girl misses her lessons she can only grow larger, and when she does so she is liable to be summoned to (unwelcome?) bed with the title Mrs, not Miss, as William Empson has pointed out in *Some Versions of Pastoral* (1935). Now, if a theriac allows you to change healths, it should also let you change names mutually, by exchange, and in the following manner. We know that Lewis Carroll is the Latinate form of Charles Lutwidge; we also know that when the Dormouse told the story of the three little girls at the bottom of a well, he called them Elsie, Lacie and Tillie. Elsie stands for Lorina's first two initials L.C.; Lacie is the anagram of Alice; and Tillie is short for Matilda, Edith's pet name. But if we make Nonsense of this, we find that L.C. are Lewis Carroll's initials, Lacie has the same consonants, and that Tillie must apply to the girl who had her hand on the tiller, who was Alice, who is L.C. amplified. Carroll, who was rowing in the bows, told Alice her own Wonderland story, and therefore was the steersman: but since he often took his cue from what she and her sisters said, they were helping to row the boat of the story also. It was only because of this that the Adventure was successful, with nobody getting snarked. (How Alice turned this exchange back on him must be left till later.)

However, as the Gnat yet again pointed out, it is no use calling people names if they don't answer to them. This is quite possible if you administer the theriac too brusquely: it may then come on with the suddenness of a thunderstorm on a Tuesday ('a very enjoyable day'), which will make you forget your name; though it may arrive in the shape of a riddle with no answer leaving you fast as lightning in your own headpiece (which is as much as to say, your title). Yet what is so bad about forgetting your name if your partner remembers it because it is now his? It all depends on the theriac being mutually administered. For though Alice took it well enough when Carroll had the Sheep address her as a little goose – the only kind he would say 'Bo!' to – when another girl called *him* 'Goosey', because he had forgotten something, he reprimanded her sharply. An even more telling anecdote comes from Isa Bowman (p. 19):

I had an idle trick of drawing caricatures when I was a child, and one day when he was writing some letters I began to make a picture of him on the back of an envelope. I quite forget what the drawing was like – probably it was an abominable libel – but suddenly he turned and saw what I was doing. He got up from his seat and turned very red, frightening me very much. Then he took my poor little drawing, and tearing it into small pieces threw it into the fire without a word. Afterwards he came suddenly to me, and saying nothing, caught me up in his arms and kissed me passionately.

Isa Bowman also says of him that 'of being photographed he had a horror' though he was an avid photographer, especially of young girls who in the end posed for him without clothes on. But if a caricature and a photograph are both theriacs of a kind, Isa's drawing seems to have acted on him more in the way of a love-potion. All this thus confirms our emended reading of Rule 19, 'Jam tomorrow, and jam yesterday, and only black draughts today.'

The concoction had in fact already been taken by Carroll long before *Looking-glass* was published, as is apparent from a poem fittingly entitled 'Stolen Waters', and dated May 9, 1862 – that is, five days after Alice's tenth birthday.

> She plucked a branch above her head,
>     With rarest fruitage laden:
> 'Drink of this juice, Sir Knight!' she said:
>     ''Tis good for Knight and maiden.'

The Knight drank the juice, which set his brain on fire, melted his soul and caused him to change hearts with the Maiden. The exchange was sealed with a kiss, which proved fatal: for it was a passionate one, and by demanding it the Maiden proved false, and in the Knight's eyes she lost her youth:

> In the gray light I saw her face,
>     And it was withered, old, and gray.

So he lost his mind and fled.

> They call me mad – I smile, I weep,
>     Uncaring how or why:
> Yea, when one's heart is laid asleep,
>     What better than to die?

The theriac, however, was at work, and by following the steps of the Lobster Quadrille became treacle in three stages. In the first stage

My heart was sad, my voice was gay,

and in the second

My voice is sad, my heart is gay,

while the third stage opened when he heard a voice sing

'*Be as a child* – '

whereupon he regained his human heart.

We shall bypass the question of whether this pre-Raphaelite-like poem was inspired by an actual event in Carroll's life.* This is not just because Carroll's diaries from April 1858 to May 1862 have been lost, but because we do not need to adduce a cause when constructing a parallel. We have, at any rate, found a child where our argument requires it to be, and we can follow its career in his friendship with Alice. Through its eyes the adult life that had been transposed into the future appeared in the form of the other characters in *Wonderland* whose hearts and voices are so often at odds, and who take up the Anglo-Saxon Attitudes that express those odds with the parts of the body, or with parts of speech, or with that murder the Hatter committed when he sang at the Queen of Hearts' Concert.

The odds can also be expressed by turning the exemplary sentiments of recitation pieces into a parody. They result in typical transformations:

'*You are old, Father William,*' *the young man said,*
'*And your hair has become very white;*
*And yet you incessantly stand on your head* –
*Do you think, at your age, it is right?*'

'*In my youth,*' *Father William replied to his son,*
'*I feared it might injure the brain;*
*But, now that I'm perfectly sure I have none,*
*Why, I do it again and again.*'**

---

*Its theme is, of course, archetypal. 'At Aberdeen in 1597, for instance, Andro Man confessed to carnal dealings with the then Queen of Elphame, who had "a grip of all the craft" . . . "She is very pleasant and will be old and young when she pleases."' (Robert Graves, *The White Goddess*, 1961.)

**Carroll's father was still alive when this was printed in *Wonderland*, in 1865, and did not die until 1868. If any particular point of reference is needed, it may not be out of place to quote this from Carroll's diary of 1862:

Preached a sermon Dec 28 at Cleasby: 2 Peter v 4 'Where is the promise of His coming? For since the fathers fell asleep, all things continue as they were until now.'

A similar situation is found in Alice's queer version of ''Tis the voice of the sluggard'. There, the Lobster, if not exactly standing on its head, at least turns out its toes by means of its nose; and that, as Alice explained, is the first position in dancing. The dance, of course, is the Lobster Quadrille, to which the whiting invites the snail; but the snail then loses its shell to become a sluggard, and is given it back again in the parody to become a lobster. Its voice is as gay as a lark when the sands are dry, but when the tide rises and sharks are around, its voice has a timid and tremulous sound. The inverted posture thus goes with a change in voice and should, following the logic of 'Stolen Waters', be accompanied by a change of heart. Instead of this, however, we find that there is a change of lobster, and we may suspect that the heart is to be found under its carapace.

One clue to this transformation is to be found in the Trial scene, where the King and Queen of Hearts are judging a case that centres around Stolen Tarts. But what kind of theft is involved here?

> '*I gave her one, they gave him two,*
> *You gave us three or more:*
> *They all returned from him to you,*
> *Though they were mine before.*'

The weight of evidence, such as it is, suggests that, like the hearts in 'Stolen Waters', they have been exchanged rather than stolen, and that Carrollian food is a temptation labelled 'EAT ME' just as the liquid theriac is one labelled 'DRINK ME', their effect being a change of size. From this, it is permissible to deduce that when heart and voice are at odds, and the voice is speaking, the heart of the matter will be expressed in terms of food and drink: that is, what the Ancients knew as Ambrosia and Nectar respectively.

We find this confirmed in the second stanza of the 'Sluggard', which recounts how the Owl and the Panther were sharing a pie, and ends with the Panther about to eat the Owl; just as Fury was about to eat the Mouse, and the Snark to execute its judgment upon the pig. The Snark itself was not to be born for another thirteen years or so, but its constituents, the snail and the shark, have already struck up an acquaintance as a result of the Lobster Quadrille and introduce the act of introjection that produces a theriac.

Having started with what seems to be a simple situation where two things that should be in accord are at odds, we find that a large number of other Anglo-Saxon Attitudes are also involved. The transposed element is to be thought of as playing a game of Musical Chairs. The losing player, however, does not quit the game nor, indeed, must he if Rule 14 is to be observed: 'To save your life, hide it in a portmanteau.' He therefore forms a partnership with one of the other players, sometimes in such circumstances that he must allow himself to be eaten up. But if this is so where, when heart and voice are at odds, does the heart find lodging within the body?

Since the odds can be expressed by an inverted posture, there seems to be only one answer: when the voice is gay, the saddened heart will have to sink into the speaker's boots,★ which must then be placed where the head should be. That the Lobster is in fact a boot as well as food is hinted at in the gloss given to the Lobster Quadrille by the Gryphon. We know for a start that the dancers change lobsters; and it is easy enough to change them from blue to red, by putting them into boiling water. However, the sea into which the Turtles throw them is apparently cold, and another agent must be found to effect the transformation. This, of course, is the whiting, who partners the lobsters: and the reason that it is called by this name is, 'Because boots and shoes under the sea are done with whiting. Now you know.'★★

---

★ 'If that be so,' she straight replied,
'Each heart with each doth coincide.
What boots it? For the world is wide.'
('The Three Voices', 1856)

★★ In his Preface to *The Hunting of the Snark*, Carroll said of the helmsman that he used to stand by with tears in his eyes when he saw the bowsprit being fastened on, anyhow, across the rudder, but could not say anything because of the Bellman's addition to Rule 42. The office of helmsman, he went on, 'was usually undertaken by the Boots, who found it a refuge from the Baker's constant complaints about the insufficient blacking of his three pairs of boots'.

We can confirm much of this from evidence given in *Wonderland* during the Trial, when the Hatter was called as witness. The Queen of Hearts then frightened him so much, by calling for the list of the singers during the last concert, that he shook off both his shoes and did not stop to put them on when dismissed.

It is easy to say that he lost heart with his shoes, but we also know that he had a cup of tea in one hand from which he bit a large piece instead of attacking the bread and butter he had in the other hand. 'Just at this moment Alice felt a very curious sensation . . . she was beginning to grow larger again.' Obviously, some elixir is working here at one remove, which we must suspect the Hatter of having anagrammatically confused: TEA turned into EAT, so that DRINK could not SHRINK. But much the same accident happened to him when he was in prison, for all he had to eat there was oyster shells. So if for 'tea-cup' we can read 'oyster shell', for 'oyster' we may read 'lobster': and as the Hatter had landed in hot water it was obviously bootless for him to appeal against his sentence.

We know that his offence was a capital one – he had murdered Time – if only because he did not take off his hat while in court. Had Tenniel inscribed the large ticket that adorned his hat with double the price, we could have explained this by saying that the Hatter, though judged by the King, was worth more than a sovereign: unfortunately the inscription reads 'In this Style 10/6', which will not do. (But the normal price for a hat in those days was 4/9, as Carroll made out in 'The Three Voices'.) We must therefore call another witness, namely Amos Judd, to remind us that the Hatter could not have been a poet or he would not have gone to prison. He cannot have worn long hair, either, for that is part of the syllogistic definition of a poet, even though this is contradicted by Tenniel's illustration. Being here at an impasse, we must call Carroll himself to the witness stand, bearing with him the description of an engraving called 'The Duett' from 'The Rectory Umbrella':

> The most casual observer cannot fail to remark what a tendency the love of music has to make the hair grow in full luxuriance, nay, he may safely conclude, if he finds no such effects produced in *him*, that he has no ear for melody.

Since the Hatter did have long hair, we must conclude that he also loved music, and that what he hated was doing Time. So why did he keep on his hat while in court? Because, to quote Ethel Arnold, Carroll 'always used to say that when the time came for him to take off his hat when he met one of his quondam child friends in the street, it was time for the friendship to cease' (*Windsor Magazine*,

ETTY. R.A. PAINTER.  THE  DUETT.  A BELL ENGRAVER.
from the picture in the Vernon Gallery

1929). For otherwise courtship should then begin, its end being
License or Banns, and rather than face that he bared his locks and
bolted like a hare.

The fate of the Hatter thus tells us what happens when you drink
too much tea, that specific 'for all the ills that flesh is heir to'. The
constant change of attitudes, especially between the vertical extremities, which it brings on was still on Carroll's mind in 1870,
according to a letter written by the Right Reverend Bishop Edward
Henry Hicks after he had dined in Christ Church: 'N.B. Heard this
evening the last new joke of the author of Alice in Wonderland.
He knows a man whose feet are so large that he has to put on his
trousers over his head.'

From which we can deduce that, if you have exchanged hearts
for food, and it sinks into your boots, and you are standing on your

head rather than eat your hat, and you are as gay as a lark as Blue changes to Pink because Black has been White-washed, you will find that your feet are shod with lobsters. The Quadrille requires you to exchange these with your partner, as being the only way that the theriac can safely work. We may rest assured, however, that the Snark will eat them up himself. What then?

*'Unerringly she pinned it down.'* (*'The Three Voices'.*)

Chapter VIII

# A Telling end

It is the Boojum that happens next, and let us bring this tale to a head. This fits in every way, down to the fact that the Boojum only appears in the last line of *The Hunting of the Snark* which was, of course, the first that came to Carroll's mind.

We have already asked about it, though not much to the purpose. We could have given Carroll's explanation at the time, but this would have been incomprehensible: for, as we said, any answer to the question depends on the language we use. We have now learnt it, by following the steps according to which an elixir is created, and by figuring out the attitudinal Quadrille taking place within the body of its maker. We can thus turn to *Sylvie and Bruno* with a good conscience and discover Carroll's etymology of 'Boojum'. The name, he said, was a portmanteau formed out of boot-jack and boot-jam: and this last is obviously what happens when you cannot get whatever it is out of your boot (which is now on the other foot) even with the aid of the Jack of Hearts.

But the appearance of the Boojum puts the whole game of Nonsense into jeopardy, for the Baker must then vanish. It in fact contradicts Rule 19, 'Jam to-morrow, and jam yesterday, but never jam *to-day*.' For

> '*if e'er by chance I put*
> *My fingers into glue,*
> *And madly squeeze a right-hand foot*
> *Into a left-hand shoe*'

the etymology of Boojum tells us that the result can only be jam all the time.*

*Sylvie and Bruno Concluded* gives us another view of the Boojum, but this time disguised, in a rather damp tale of the three little Foxes who were put into a picnic hamper to stop them from eating a lamb. First they ate the food in the hamper, and then the second little Fox ate the third little Fox, and then the first little Fox ate the second. When the hamper was opened, there was nothing in it at all. '"Eldest

---

*The reader may spread it on a tart, if he is willing to be brought up in Court. But he should realise that in the 1860s 'tart' was a term of endearment and not, as now, of reproach.

little Fox, have you been eating *yourself*, you wicked little Fox?"
And the eldest little Fox said "Whihuauch!" And then Bruno saw
there was only its *mouth* in the hamper! So he took the mouth, and
he opened it, and shook, and shook! And at last he shook the little
Fox out of its own mouth!'

There can be little doubt that the same fate overtakes the Snark
whenever it succumbs to the urge to eat its own boots. It then
becomes a Boojum, having swallowed all the odds that are part of
itself. No wonder then that it was the Baker, with his three pairs
of boots, who was surprised by this activity and vanished inside it
with that 'Boo – !' which so aptly echoes the melancholy words
of the Mock Turtle's last song:

> 'Beau – ootiful Soo – oop!
> Beau – ootiful Soo – oop!'

For the speciality of the Baker (who, we must also remember, had
forgotten his own name) was Bridecake,

> . . . for which, I may state,
> No materials were to be had.

They were, of course, in his boots. Why three pairs? We shall
come to them soon: but now we need only remember what the
Butcher said to the Beaver, 'The proof is complete / If only I've stated
it thrice.'★

We may say that we have done the same: we have made the
Riddle disappear into a surd, into a portmanteau, and into the
Boojum. As to the thesis we have proved, we cannot do better than
go back to Wittgenstein:

---

★ The Butcher's problem can perhaps be understood as an example 'in
ordinary Double Rule of Three'. Carroll describes the logic of this Rule in
the Appendix to Knot VII, *A Tangled Tale*:

> Now, from *two* equations only, we cannot find, *separately*, the values of
> *three* unknowns: certain *combinations* of them, however, may be found.
> Also we know that we can, by the help of the given equations, eliminate
> 2 of the 3 unknowns from the quantity whose value is required, which
> will then contain one only. If, then, the required value is ascertainable
> at all, it can only be by the 3rd unknown vanishing of itself: otherwise
> the problem is impossible.

He takes this up in *Sylvie and Bruno*, where the narrator is told: 'Have you
never heard that two is company, and – '; while later in the same book he
mentions how the Purse of Fortunatus (known to us as a Klein Bottle) can
be made of three handkerchiefs. The result? 'Whatever is *inside* the Purse
is *outside* it; and whatever is *outside* it, is *inside* it.'

This book will perhaps only be understood by those who have themselves already thought the thoughts which are expressed in it – or similar thoughts. It is therefore not a text-book. Its object would be attained if it afforded pleasure to one who read it with understanding.

The book deals with the problems of philosophy and shows, as I believe, that the method of formulating these problems rests on the misunderstanding of the logic of our language. Its whole meaning could be summed up as follows: What can be said at all can be said clearly; and whereof one cannot speak, thereof one must be silent.

We have taken philosophy in its widest application, as referring to the meaning of life. Carroll asked two rhetorical questions about *that*: the first, 'Life, what is it but a dream?' and the second, 'Is not Life itself a Paradox?' It only remains for us to ask a third question, 'Is Life Nonsense?' to give full weight to the enormity of our thesis. For while it cannot now be in doubt that Carroll's Nonsense was life to him, to answer the question properly we must put it in front of the looking-glass and ask 'Is Nonsense Death?'

This question was in fact broached after recording Rule 19, via Mr Gorham's peculiar view of Baptism. We said then that Carroll's method of dealing with the Rule was unorthodox enough to have had some unexpected results, and that the Rule is strangely bound up with the answer he gave to the Riddle. We can now substantiate those remarks.

Returning to Mr Gorham, we have shown that his view of Baptism is workable only if the water used is a theriac, and the persons involved in the sacrament are in a state of mutuality. This is not so much a paradox as an open secret, 'and the name of the secret is Love'. But we also suggested that the taking of a theriac can lead to addiction, the transpositions it involves tempting the drinker to swallow himself under the illusion that he is taking part in a mutual exchange. The fatality is in fact foreshadowed in 'Lanrick: A Game For Two Players', that Carroll published in 1893. In it we find his Rule 9,★ which shall be our

Rule 20. 'When a Player has only one man left, he has lost the Game.'

This is the opposite of our first Rule, whose position as the oldest one in the book is made clear at the start of both the *Alices*. In *Wonderland* we read that Alice 'once tried to box her own ears for having cheated herself in a game of croquet she was playing against

---

★ 'May 18 1881. Tried the new rules for "Lanrick" with Bayne. The game is still apt to be uninteresting when one player has only one man.'

herself, for this curious child was very fond of pretending to be two people'. The well of fancy would be useless without this pretence, and it can include more than two. For in *Looking-glass* Alice remembered having had an argument with her sister, 'all because Alice had begun with "Let's pretend we're kings and queens"; and her sister, who liked being very exact, had argued that they couldn't because there were only two of them, and Alice had been reduced at last to say, "Well, *you* can be one of them, then, and *I'll* be all the rest."'

When a Player has only one man left, he has lost the Game. Here is a three-fold proof that Carroll lost the Game – which is only the other way of saying that he lived in Nonsense until he died. The proof, or demonstration, has to do with his relations to Alice. It is more than likely that she was not playing his game all the time, for while the Dodgson family motto was '*Respice et Resipice*' ('Look back and recover your senses') the original Liddell motto was '*Unus et idem*' ('One and the same'). In any case, we must remember that Carroll wrote to her, when she was 39, that he could scarcely picture her to himself as more than 7 years old. But his spell could not stop her from growing, and his attentions having been early disapproved of by Mrs Liddell, it might be said that he deserted her.★ Then, when she was 28 and after a long engagement, she married Robert Hargreaves. Carroll did not go to the wedding, which took place on September 15, 1880. He had graver matters to attend to: his aunt Lucy Lutwidge, who had been keeping house for the Dodgson children after their mother's death, died in the first week of that month. Carroll went down to Guildford on September 4 to see her before she died, stayed for her funeral on the 8th, and departed for Eastbourne on the following day. This sequence of events curiously echoes another twenty-nine years earlier, when Carroll came formally into residence at Christ Church on January 24, 1851, and his mother died on the 26th: so that he had to return to Croft on either that or the succeeding day, which was his nineteenth birthday. If we are looking for the way that the character of the Baker began to form itself in his mind, the nature of these two occasions can not be ignored.

---

★ 'May 12 1864. During the last few days I have applied in vain for leave to take the children on the river, i.e. Alice, Edith and Rhoda: but Mrs. Liddell will not let *any* come in future – rather superfluous caution!'

'May 11 1865. Met Alice and Miss Prickett (the governess) in the quadrangle: Alice seems changed a good deal, and hardly for the better – probably going through the usual awkward age of transition.'

*'Here may the silent tears I weep*
*Lull the vexed spirit into rest,*
*As infants sob themselves asleep*
*Upon their mother's breast.'*
*('Solitude'.)*

The Baker, it will be remembered, had forgotten his name. However, he did say that he had been called after a dear uncle of his: and, putting him into Carroll's shoes, we might suppose that he was called either Hassard Dodgson, Skeffington Lutwidge or Charles Henry Lutwidge. Or, since the dear uncle was of major importance, was he just called Charles Lutwidge? Charles Lutwidge it must be: and this allows us to show the three pairs of boots in Carroll's ancestry, each pair corresponding to a Dodgson and a Lutwidge:

Right Reverend
Charles Dodgson          Henry Lutwidge    Charles Lutwidge

Captain Charles  Elizabeth Anne Dodgson = Major Charles
   Dodgson                                      Lutwidge

The Venerable
Charles Dodgson = Frances Jane Lutwidge   Charles Henry Lutwidge

      Charles Lutwidge Dodgson

Taking 'Charles' as a foot, 'Dodgson' as the right-hand shoe and 'Lutwidge' as the left-hand one, 'Lewis Carroll' – which is Charles Lutwidge reversed into Latin – then records the squeezing of one right-hand foot into one left-hand shoe, and of one left-hand foot into one right-hand shoe. It was this genealogical Quadrille that

125

produced the theriacally-minded Dodgson, down to the fact that it 'reversed the line' in the third generation: for both Captain Charles Dodgson and Major Charles Lutwidge are simultaneously Carroll's grandfathers and great-uncles. Calling to mind what we know of the avuncular relation between Carroll and his girl friends, and its similarity to the wriggling Knight's move in chess, we may not only suspect that he was aware of this, but prove so with his backward-reading letter: 'the only "Uncle Dodgson", that was alive *then*, was my *grandfather.*'

But *why* did the Baker forget his name when its two parts were thus paired off in his ancestry? If it had been a portmanteau – which on the face of it was not impossible, seeing that he was one himself in wearing seven coats at the same time – we would conclude that it had been left behind on shore when the ship sailed amongst his 42 pieces of luggage. *Sylvie and Bruno* tells us that we are on the right track here:

> 'And *what* did you say his name was?' said the Vice-Warden. The Professor referred to a card he held in his hand. 'His Adiposity The Baron Doppelgeist.'
> 'Why does he come with such a funny name?' said my Lady.
> 'He couldn't well change it on the journey,' the Professor meekly replied, 'because of the luggage.'

But since his name wasn't exactly a portmanteau we need another reason, which emerges if we discover how the luggage came to be left on shore in the first place: it must have been labelled with seven addresses, while he had signed on under a *nom-de-plume*★ that sailed back to front.

From whose wing was this *nom-de-plume* taken but from the raven's? For of inspired birds, as the Reverend K. Macaulay wrote in *The Story of St. Kilda* (1794), 'ravens were accounted the most prophetical. Accordingly, to have the foresight of a raven is to this

---

★ '"It's part of the Conspiracy, Love! One must have an alias, you know!"' (*Sylvie and Bruno*, Chapter IX.) Dodgson used a number of pen names during his life. He proposed 'Dares', from his birthplace Daresbury, to the editor of 'College Rhymes', together with 'Edgar Cuthwellis' and 'Edgar U. C. Westhill' (both anagrams of 'Charles Lutwidge'), 'Louis Carroll' and 'Lewis Carroll': and the editor chose wisely. Before this he had used 'B.B.'; 'K', perhaps because it is the eleventh letter in the alphabet; 'Ch.Ch.', no doubt for the Charles who lived in Christ Church; 'C.L.D.' for serious poems, these being his proper initials; and 'R.W.G.', which are the fourth letters in his three real names. Why the fourth letter? The answer must be, Because the fourth letter in 'Dodgson' is a surd: the name is pronounced 'Dodson'.

*Alice Liddell. C.L.D's last photograph of her.*

day a proverbial expression, denoting a preternatural sagacity in predicting fortuitous events.' Since *The Hunting of the Snark* was written in 1876, we must therefore look for an event in the future that will cause the Baker to forget his name: and this is to be found as the consequence of Alice's marriage in 1880, for she then turned 'Carroll' back from a surname into a Christian name, by naming her first child 'Caryl'. Moreover, as Caryl Hargreaves★ wrote many years later, 'When she asked him to be godfather to her *son*, he characteristically failed to reply.' ('Lewis Carroll as recalled by Alice', *New York Times*, May 1, 1932.)

The proof was completed seventeen years later, when he himself disavowed his *nom-de-plume*, and Rule 20 came into force almost immediately. As Charles Dodgson, he had always disliked being addressed by members of the public as 'Lewis Carroll', and went so far as to send a printed circular to misguided correspondents, telling them that the address of his *alter ego* was care of its publishers. Finally, on November 8, 1897, he wrote in his diary:

> A letter came, addressed to 'L. Carroll, Christ Church, Oxford.' So many such now come, that I have decided to *refuse* them, and gave it, unopened, to Telling, to return to the Post Office. All such will now go back to the writers, through the Dead Letter Office, with endorsement 'not known'.

If we were to read this entry superficially, as a plain avowal that Dodgson was no longer interested in Carroll, we would do no more than many another sensible commentator. Let us rather make Nonsense of it, by remembering the Definition which begins his *Dynamics of a Parti-cle*:

> PLAIN SUPERFICIALITY is the character of a speech in which any two points being taken, the speaker is found to lie wholly with regard to those two points.

This definition allowed us to set down our Rule 5, and it is still incumbent on us not to be deceived by an appearance, however sensible it appears. Carroll's entry of November 8, 1897, in fact introduces one of the most baffling Pillow Problems that could be devised, and it provides us with his final comment upon the Riddle whose fairly appropriate answer he had published the year before. For, given that a raven is like a writing-desk because of something said that cannot be allowed, what are the odds against the name

---

★ Caryl Hargreaves eventually became a Captain. This is of some interest in working out the genealogical Quadrille, because the ecclesiastical line between Carroll and his great-great-grandfather had been broken by his Dodgson grandfather and great-uncle, who became a Captain, and by his Lutwidge great-uncle and grandfather, who became a Major. However, the Captain died young, and his widow married a clergyman; it was also a clergyman that her sister Mary married, her daughter being Menella Smedley. The martial strain was excluded from Carroll's immediate family: he, Skeffington and Edwin were all ordained, thus following in the footsteps of the Bishop rather than the Baronet.

of the college porter being Telling at the time when Dodgson refused to be in any further correspondence with Carroll?

The answer is incalculable, except in terms of Nonsense. Carroll is to Dodgson much as a corollary is to a Euclidean proof: both are flukes, that convert chance into order and so make a coincidence earn its living. If, following the lead given us in the account of Watkins H. Williams's tutorial, we look at this entry as an incident in a game of billiards, we can appreciate Carroll's cool and triumphant delight in finding that his great opponent, Time, had left his ball, in the form of Telling, just where he could bring off a cannon. As a master geometrician, he was long accustomed to calculate the tangents involved: and not only did he bring off the cannon, but the stroke to end all strokes, and with a regular Crow holed his own, his opponent's, and the red ball as well.

The table thus cleared, Dodgson had but one man left, namely himself: and, true to the rule, he died nearly ten weeks later, on January 14, 1898. But to prove that he died as he lived, a master of Nonsense, we must be more exact than this. The rule he followed on his last day must be our Rule 20, the negative of our Rule 19 and of his Rule 42. What is it about 42?

> 'Let me see: four times five is twelve, and four times six is thirteen, and four times seven is – oh dear! I shall never get to twenty at that rate!'

Twenty *seems* reachable when you multiply 4 by 13 on scale 42 – but the appearance is, of course, deceptive. What then happens is that all is at sixes and sevens, whether you add or multiply them: and, as Carroll told us, when A and B are in that state, the problem is to tell how much reading they do during the Eights. The answer, of course, is 'None', as his diary entry for the 8th of November states.

Let us continue to be exact, however Nonsensical this makes us. November is the eleventh month of the year, and adding that to the date we have a total of 19. This is a fluke. So is the fact that between November 8, 1897 and January 14, 1898, when he died, there are 67 days. But can it also be a fluke that he died 13 days before his birthday on January 27? (He then would have been only 66, but it would have been his 67th *birthday*.) And what are we to make of the fact that 67 is a prime number and the 19th in order of magnitude?★

The nature of this problem is so intractable to Reason that we shall restrict our comments on it to recording the events of Carroll's

---

★In the interests of Nonsense I must add that these lines were written in 1974, 76 years after Carroll's death; and that 76 is the product of 4 × 19.

last days. On January 5, 1898, he received a telegram telling him that the husband of his sister Charlotte had died. This was the twelfth Charles, the Reverend C. S. Collingwood. Dodgson was then at Guildford at the family house 'The Chestnuts', and wished to go to the funeral, but was himself stricken by influenza. On the advice of the family physician (whose name, Dr Gabb, is another telling coincidence) he took to his bed. There bronchitis set in and his liability to respiratory ailments became fatal. A few days before he died he confessed to one of his sisters that his illness was a great trial to his patience, and asked another one to read aloud the hymn whose every stanza ends 'Thy will be done'. On January 13 he spoke the last words that have been recorded from him: 'Take away those pillows – I shall need them no more.'

> The end came about half-past two on the afternoon of the 14th. One of his sisters was in the room at the time and she only noticed that the hard breathing suddenly ceased. The nurse, whom she summoned, at first hoped that this was a sign that he had taken a turn for the better. And so, indeed, he had . . .
>
> (Collingwood, *Life and Letters*, p. 348)

We have no reason to think otherwise, and reference to Hone's *Every Day Book*, which contains the pictorial original of the Jabberwock, bears this judgment out. For January 14, which is marked there as being the beginning of the Oxford Lenten Term – and Lent is, of course, the time to go on a fast – is also the day of St Felix.★ Hone records of this saint that 'According to the Legend, his Body, for ages after his death, distilled a liquor that cured diseases.'

---

★Carroll owned another, later almanac like Hone's: Chambers's *Book of Days*. Its entry for January 14 commemorates the death of Bishop Berkeley, philosopher and mathematician, and it notices his once notorious work: *Siris, A Chain of Philosophical Reflexions and Inquiries Concerning the Virtues of Tar-water*.

Intermission

# The absurd

C. L. Dodgson's grave is in Guildford cemetery. It is marked by a white cross bearing his name, and common sense might hold that it should also mark the end of our enquiry. But there are two good reasons for not ending here. The first is to be found in *A New Theory of Parallels*, where Dodgson raised what in this context is an eschatological problem. His words, already quoted, are worth repeating:

> When we come to the limit, what then? What do we come to? There must be either Something, or Nothing. . . . That there should be neither of these is absurd.

The second reason is that the white cross also bears the name of Lewis Carroll, who surely would have made Nonsense of this proposition. Indeed, have we not ourselves done so from the start, by defining the absurd *as* the limit?

For a Nonsense Master the absurd is also the result of putting a surd to work on the spur of the moment and according to the rules, while being logical in a self-contradictory fashion, turning the odds to his own advantage and, by making oppositely acting forces exchange partners, forming them into a Couple, a portmanteau or a black draught. True, it now seems as though this draught has come from the Styx, whose ferryman normally plies in one direction only – from Something to Nothing. But how if the passenger has a return ticket?

Carroll described this journey (made with a map anyone can understand) in *The Hunting of the Snark*. There he also gave an account of the natural history of the surd, the various ways to capture it, and the fatal attraction it exerts on an alliterative series of hunters up to the moment when one of them reaches the limit and vanishes. What then?

131

Our best answer is via Humpty Dumpty's 'Impenetrability!' This conversation stopper, as we noted in Chapter VI, originated with Professor Bartholomew Price, who held that it was impossible for two particles of matter to occupy the same space at the same time. But we then showed that this cannot hold good for Nonsense, whose particles are mutually inclusive rather than mutually exclusive. If the Baker has vanished, therefore, we may yet find him deep in this kind of preoccupation.

Carroll always held that he had no idea what the Boojum looked like, and indeed refused to publish Holiday's impermissibly factual drawing of it. This was wise, on at least two counts: we really cannot expect to picture a surd that swallows everything at odds with it, ending with itself; and even if we could, would *we* not vanish the moment we saw it? This is not entirely an academic question, though to get its full flavour we must also ask: Has the Baker vanished for good?★

If 'to vanish' means 'to be turned into a surd', which is a literal enough description of what happened to the Baker, the answer is: No, he does not vanish for good. The *Snark*, of course, is pessimistically silent on this point. But in the golden weather of *Wonderland* Carroll was sufficiently master of the situation to have the Cheshire Cat vanish *and* reappear, several times, and at will. Why then should the Baker not do likewise? All he need do is observe how the Cat lets its mouth appear before the rest of it, and leaves a grin behind when it vanishes. Like the eldest little Fox, then, the Baker will reappear if shaken out of himself. This will naturally be a one-sided affair, for we know that the third unmistakable mark of a Snark – that is, of a surd that is not yet totally introverted – is its inability to take a jest. But as for *making* a jest – why, that's quite a different proposition.

---

★ The eschatological problem here is nicely summed up in a letter Dodgson wrote to Edith Rix in 1885:

> One subject you touched on – 'the Resurrection of the Body' – is very interesting to me. *My* conclusion was to give up the *literal* meaning of the *material* body altogether . . . the actual *material* usable for *physical* bodies has been used over and over again, so that each atom would have several owners. The mere solitary fact of the existence of *cannibalism* is to my mind a sufficient *reductio ad absurdum* of the theory that the particular set of atoms I shall happen to own at death . . . will be mine in the next life.

The Carrollian view could well be that one set of atoms could form a portmanteau of its several owners. This is a respectable animistic doctrine, but not one we need pursue.

It is this proposition that allows us to continue, and to show that the question about the Baker's vanishing is not just of academic interest. For what kind of surd is it that makes mischief, plays with appearances, revels in dancing and, like the Snark, has a flavour of Will-o'-the-wisp? The answer is to be found in the title Carroll thought of giving *Alice's Adventures* after he had decided against *Underground*, and before Dean Liddell had suggested *in Wonderland*. It is the kind of surd that carries one off by making the head spin, and it lives *in Elfland*.★

---

★ As Campbell of Tiree will tell us:

In this climate the eddies are among the most curious of natural phenomena. On calm summer days they go past, whirling above straws and dust, and as not another breath of wind is moving at the same time their cause is sufficiently puzzling. In Gaelic the eddy is known as 'the people's puff of wind' and its motion 'Travelling on tall grass stems'. By throwing one's left shoe at it, the fairies are made to drop whatever they may be taking away – men, women, children, or animals.

(*Superstitions of the Highlands and Islands*, 1900)

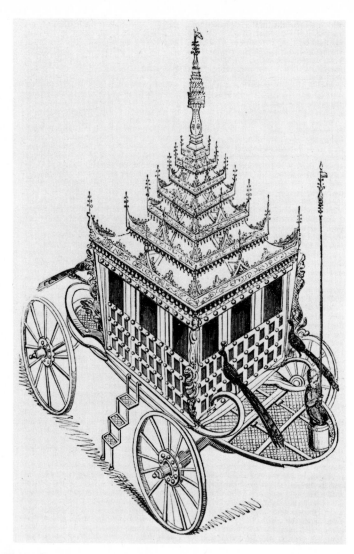

*The Rath, or Burmese Imperial State Carriage; captured, in September 1825, at Tavoy, a seaport in the Burmese Empire. (Hone's Every Day Book for Nov 28.)*

# Chapter IX

# The Double

> The next question is, what is the best time for seeing Fairies?
> I believe I can tell you all about that.
>   The first rule is, that it must be a *very* hot day – that we may
> consider as settled: and you must be just a *little* sleepy – but not
> too sleepy to keep your eyes open, mind. Well, and you ought
> to feel a little – what one may call 'fairyish' – the Scotch call it
> 'eerie', and perhaps that's a prettier word.
>
> (Sylvie and Bruno, Chapter XIV)

Carroll followed these rules strictly enough at the opening of
*Wonderland*, for he there says that the hot day made Alice feel very
sleepy and stupid: and what did she see then but a White Rabbit
that took a watch out of its waistcoat pocket. It was late – too late –
on the afternoon of July 4, 1862.

But where are the elves, as we have already asked?

Let us not jump to conclusions about the White Rabbit or any
of the other curious creatures in the *Alices*. First let us remember
the tradition according to which elves and their congeners live
under the earth, in fairy duns; and that it is winter there when it is
summer for us, while one of their days lasts a year by our time, and
vice versa. It will also be fine weather for them when there are
clouds in our skies: and this must explain the unexpected fact that
the weather records show the afternoon of July 4, 1862, to have been
overcast and rather cool.

There is no knowing when the tradition started, and it is highly
unlikely to come to an end in spite of all that Reason can say against
it. Indeed, it is partly because Reason exists that the tradition continues, if only as its mirror image. Therefore, as the one develops,
so will the other: sometimes as its heretical alternative and sometimes Nonsensically in inverse cooperation. Elves are thus contrary
beings, as they must be if they exist between Something and Nothing.
As for the nature of their existence, it is found via the Irish name
for a fairy dun, a *rath*, which is etymologically connected with
*wraith*.

With this in mind, let us consider the mome rath that appears in
*Wonderland* as the Duchess's baby, not forgetting the Duchess herself
and her talk about axes. The extraordinary behaviour of these two
characters has been examined by C. W. Scott-Giles, OBE, Fitzalan

Pursuivant of Arms Extraordinary, who was understandably puzzled by the absence of the Duchess's husband.

> An answer to the question, 'Where was Alice's Duke?' can be found if we consider the identity of the baby. A duke's son who turned into a pig – who can this be but Richard of Gloucester who came to the throne as Richard III, took the white boar as his badge, and was called 'the hog' in political lampoons?
>
> (Quoted in R. L. Green's edition of the *Alices*, p. 257)

If we now turn to Shakespeare – as we may well do, since Carroll owned seven sets of Shakespeare at the time of his death – this supposition is confirmed. We find there that Richard is likened to an 'elvish mark'd, abortive, rooting hog'; that the first victim of his machinations was George, Duke of Clarence, who says of the then king Edward IV that 'He hearkens after prophecies and dreams / And from the cross-row plucks the letter G.' Finally, at Bosworth Field when Stanley refuses to come to Richard's aid, Richard cries, 'Off with his son George's head!'

Talk about axes!* We can also talk about plucking the letter G not only from the cross-row, as the alphabet was then called, but from *Dodgson*; and, more to the point, about Richard being elvish marked. This can only mean that he was a changeling – an elf-child or oaf, left in place of the human child the elves had stolen from his mother.

---

*This talk, as we shall see, is based on a pun; and a pun, as we have said, is the linguistic equivalent of a coincidence. This, in turn, can be thought of as an elvish prank, and we may here note a particularly odd one that was played on Carroll around his birthday on January 27. The evidence is drawn from two books that he owned, namely Hone's *Every Day Book* and Chambers's *Book of Days*, which give us the following list of dates:

January 17  St Anthony's Day, and the pictorial origin of the Jabberwock.
   21  Louis XVI executed in the 19th year of his reign, 1793.
   28  Charlemagne died, 814.
     Henry VIII died, 1547.
   29  George III died, 1820, having been mad for most of his reign.
   30  Charles I executed, 1649.
     Charles Stuart died, 1788.

The prank then played on Lewis Carroll (that is, Charles Lutwidge) is given a further twist by what Hone has to say about Charles I:

> Then he asked the executioner for his cap, which, when he had put on, he said to the executioner, 'Does my hair trouble you?' who desiring it might all be put up under his cap, it was put up by the bishop and the executioner.

It was of course when a girl put her hair up that Carroll stopped being

**NOVEMBER.**

friendly with her, for fear that they might both lose their heads. In addition, Isa Bowman records that he wore his hair somewhat longer than was then fashionable; and we have found that the Hatter, who also did, is in flagrant contradiction of poetic logic in the Amos Judd syllogism. We must then suppose that both Carroll and the Hatter were not ordinary citizens but royalty travelling incognito, whose hair would be put up if they were discovered. Both of them wore toppers, no doubt to forestall their being 'topped'. The Hatter carried this so far that he did not take off his topper in court. Our explanation for this must now be that he was anxious to disguise the fact that he was the heir apparent.

137

Elves are notorious thieves of lovely children, apparently because they cannot propagate their race by marrying amongst themselves. European folklore is unanimous in stating that their infants, which they leave in exchange, are hideous, shrivelled, bad-tempered and generally frightful; that though apparently young they are in fact extremely old; also that they have ravenous appetites. Martin Luther tells of one in his *Colloquia Mensalia*, and says that 'it would eat as much as two threshers, would laugh and be joyful when any evil happened in the home, but would cry and be very sad when all went well'.

This is a tolerably exact description of His Imperial Fatness Prince Uggug. He appears in *Sylvie and Bruno*, an elaborate and often ramshackle book whose characters are made to live now in this world, now in 'Outland'. Sylvie and Bruno are the children of the Warden of Outland, who has been invited to become King of Elfland. He therefore leaves them and the affairs of the country to the Sub-Warden, who is promoted to the status of a Vice. But he and his wife have imperial ambitions, and also try to convince the Elfin ambassador, His Adiposity the Baron Doppelgeist, that Uggug is the heir apparent. Luckily, their attempt to substitute him for the good, the clever and the beautiful Bruno is frustrated by Uggug's greed and bad temper, for on his birthday he turns into that kind of a pig known as a porcupine. 'See', says the Professor, 'the fate of a loveless life.'

The presence of elves in *Wonderland* can therefore be deduced from the changeling they left behind in place of the Duchess's baby. But here is a complication, for the child taken into Elfland is a girl, not a boy. What does this mean?

There is plentiful evidence that Carroll disliked babies of both sexes. But though boys did not improve as they grew up, in his estimation, girls did. This is not to say that girls are immune from change. One kind we have repeatedly mentioned, as summed up in a diary entry for 1865: 'Alice seems changed a good deal, and hardly for the better – probably going through the usual awkward age of transition.' Another, more germane at this moment, occurs after the White Queen has turned into a Sheep and Alice has been turning around in her shop like a teetotum. The Sheep is sitting behind the counter, knitting with more and more needles – she finally has fourteen pairs in her hands at once, a nitwittish thing to do. These, which have set a yarn into rows, then turn into oars, and Alice is given a pair to row with, the Sheep admonishing her with cries of 'Feather' as she does so.

'*Why* do you say "feather" so often?' Alice asked at last, rather vexed. 'I'm not a bird!'

'You are,' said the Sheep: 'you're a little goose.'

This transformation leads us directly back to the Riddle. For on the writing-desk, before the invention of the steel nib, what would have been dipped into its ink-well but a goose-quill? Our suspicion that Alice's simplicity was not only goosed but plucked is oddly confirmed by what happens next: she picks scented rushes. These are not exactly reeds, but like enough to be often mistaken for them: and not only is *reed* the old name for a pen, but so is its Latin equivalent, *calamus*.

The rule for a changeling then is that a boy is always a pig, and if fretful can also become quilled like the porpentine; while a girl can be written down as a goose, but need not remain one. Who, then, is the Duchess's baby? The explanation must be that if Alice is to go into Elfland, Dodgson must turn into Carroll. He does so, not by losing his temper, but by Nonsensically raving: whereupon his mirror-image flies backwards as a mome rath.

This process is inextricably bound up with the 'eerie' feeling, which Carroll seems to have fostered by being notably abstemious at table, as Isa Bowman (p. 72) records:

> I could not understand how a big grown-up man could live on a glass of sherry and a biscuit at dinner time. It seemed such a pity when there was lots of mutton and pudding that he should not have any. I always used to ask him, 'Aren't you hungry, uncle, even today?'

Obviously not, since his appetite was rather for a tonic whose effect was *almost* physical. But even here he was abstemious, for as he wrote when invited to meet a child, 'I am not omnivorous, like a pig. I like to pick and choose.'

The eerie state, as Carroll wrote, was in the Scotch tradition. He may have learnt this from his friend George MacDonald, whose books are full of fairies and magic mirrors, and whose son Greville, then aged 6, waxed so enthusiastic over the original manuscript of *Wonderland* that Carroll decided to publish it. But for a traditional account of elves and second sight we cannot do better than consult the book written in 1691 by Robert Kirk, Minister of Abersoill, and republished by Andrew Lang in 1893 under the title *The Secret Commonwealth of Elves Fauns and Fairies*. Kirk says of elves that they are subterraneans, and often thought to be the shades of the dead; and of Seers, that they can descry the Reflex or Co-Walker of a man. Seers also avouch that

> a Heluo, or Great-eater, hath a voracious Elve to be his attender, called a Joint-eater or Just-Halver, feeding on the Pith or Quintessence of what a man eats; and that thereafter he continues lean

or like a Hawke or Heron, notwith standing his devouring Appetite.

In this light Carroll appears as a Seer, whose reflex in the looking-glass reminds him of the Great-eating Doppelgeist he has refused to be. That this elf is also called a Joint-eater points to those agues brought on Caliban by urchins – the old name for both hedgehogs

and elves – when he was disobedient. Carroll likewise suffered from rheumatic cramps, and so does the Professor in *Sylvie and Bruno*. This Professor, who is the fairy equivalent of Mein Herr, the German sage, has a brother called The Other Professor, apparently Carroll's reflex. This Other remarks:

'The action of the nerves is curiously slow in some people. I had a friend, once, that if you burnt him with a red-hot poker, it would take years and years before he felt it!'
'And if you only *pinched* him?' queried Sylvie.
'Then it would take ever so much longer, of course. In fact, I doubt if the man *himself* would ever feel it. His grandchildren might.'

Whereupon Bruno says that he wouldn't like to be the grandchild of a pinched grandfather, for it might come just when you wanted to be happy. And which of Carroll's grandfathers must have been pinched for him to have his foot jammed in the wrong shoe, we cannot tell: though perhaps it was his Dodgson one, the Captain, who was killed in an Irish uprising.

Nor do we know how Carroll came to be a Seer. However, what Kirk says on this matter is again to the point, since it describes two major Anglo-Saxon Attitudes. The novice, who first ties a rope that has bound a corpse to the bier around his middle, must then

> bow his Head downwards, as did Elijah, I Kings, 18.42. and look back through his legs untill he sie a Funerall advance till the People cross two Marches: or look thus back thorough a Hole where was a Knot of Fir. But if the Wind change Points while the Hair Tedder is ty'd about him, he is in peril of his Lyfe. The usewall Method for a curious Person to get a transient sight of this otherwise invisible Crew of Subterraneans, (if impotently or rashly sought,) is to put his left Foot under the Wizard's right Foot, and the Seer's Hand is put on the Inquirer's Head who is to look over the Wizard's right Shoulder.

The draught that comes out of a knot-hole, rather than whirling straws and dust in the open air, must be left to the next chapter. But the last prescription suggests that Carroll became a Seer by being his own Wizard; for how else can we explain his elvish knack of taking a girl through the looking-glass?★

Entry into Elfland is usually effected at twilight, at either the solstices or the equinoxes. To get in at any other time a man needs a double-ended corkscrew, that is, a complete set of Anglo-Saxon

---

★ Carroll would thus have been a Warden of Outland, and as such might have been invited to occupy the Elfin throne. In *The White Goddess*, Robert Graves has this to say about the title he would then assume:

> The Danish *Ellerkonge* is the alder king, Bran, who carries off children to the other world: but *elle* also means 'elf' which should be regarded as a *cléthrad*, or alder Fairy. Thus in Goethe's well-known ballad . . . Ellerkonge is correctly translated as 'Erlkönig', the commoner German word for alder being *erle*.

Graves also says of Bran that his name means 'Raven' as well as 'alder', and that after being wounded in the heel by a poisoned dart he was beheaded; also that his head continues to sing and prophesy. I may add that children still commemorate this miracle in the riddling verse:

> King Charles the First walked and talked
> Half an hour after his head was cut off.

Attitudes. This is because the boundary between Elfland and our world cannot be apprehended in itself: it is marked only by a wraith or, what amounts to the same thing, a surd. We have found the legal equivalent of the surd to be the mute, one who does not plead his own case, and this is also true at the boundary of Elfland. What the mute does there is to plead the cause of one of the elementals. We have this on Carroll's own authority, in the first poem recorded from his pen. He was thirteen at the time, and he called the poem

## MY FAIRY

I have a fairy by my side
    Which says I must not sleep.
When once in pain I loudly cried
    It said 'You must not weep'.

If, full of mirth, I smile and grin,
    It says, 'You must not laugh';
When once I wished to drink some gin
    It said, 'You must not quaff'.

When once a meal I wished to taste
    It said 'You must not bite';
When to the wars I went in haste
    It said 'You must not fight'.

'What may I do?' at length I cried,
    Tired of the painful task.
The fairy quietly replied,
    And said 'You must not ask'.

*Moral*: 'You mustn't.'

Nineteen years later this exorbitant Joint-eater reappeared as the Duchess, who was so fond of finding morals in things – e.g. 'flamingoes and mustard both bite. And the moral of that is – "Birds of a feather flock together."' When Alice said that mustard wasn't a bird but a mineral, the Duchess had no difficulty in inventing a mustard-mine, whose moral is: 'The more there is of mine, the less there is of yours.' To find the surd in this, we must wait until the Duchess's voice died away at the start of her favourite word 'm—', as the Queen of Hearts gives her fair warning: 'Either you or your head must be off, and that in about half no time! Take your choice.' It then appears as 'not', after you have divided 'no time' into equal halves and taken it by the forelock.

More details can be found in 'Phantasmagoria'. The narrator, a
man of 42, comes home too late to dine, though supper is waiting
in the study.

> There was a strangeness in the room
> And Something white and wavy
> Was standing near me in the gloom –

which presently begins to shiver and to sneeze. It is a Ghost – not a
Spectre, the nobility of the clan which has 'first choice, by right,
In filling up a vacancy', but a Phantom, who only has second choice.
It consents to eat its host's supper, but is contrary enough to criticise
the food and the arrangements when it has finished: and on finding
that its host is not called Tibbs, as it had expected, but Tibbets, it
flies into a great rage. But before this it had been obliging enough
to give an account of its 'Nouryture', viz., its family.

> 'My father was a Brownie, Sir;
> My mother was a Fairy.
> The notion had occurred to her
> The children would be happier
> If they were taught to vary.'

To which end she produced, in order, a Pixy, two Fays, a Banshee,
a Fetch, a Kelpie, a Poltergeist, a Ghoul, two Trolls, a Goblin, a
Double, an Elf, the Phantom itself and a Leprechaun. This makes
fifteen in all, though only thirteen kinds of sprite are mentioned.     143

The question then is, can we put this family into parallel with Carroll's own, which only numbered eleven?

Perhaps. For the eleventh kind of sprite is, fittingly, the elf or changeling: and he therefore may be seen in the light of those lessons that end with a holiday on the eleventh day, and with the chess problem that is posed at the start of *Looking-glass* as 'White Pawn (Alice) to play, and win in eleven moves.'* The Phantom, who is the twelfth kind of sprite, then seems to be some sort of answer to Alice's question 'How do you manage on the twelfth?' – for it has an executive function, as expressed in its farewell to the Tibbs-who-wasn't in the words 'Good-night, old Turnip-top, good-night!'

'A nod, and he was gone.' True, the Leprechaun remains to be explained as the *last* child: and this is easy enough to do, if we remember its traditional occupation of making shoes.

But the parallel between the Dodgson and the Phantom families is not easy to maintain. Can an archdeacon really be described as 'a drudging domestic goblin', as a Brownie is defined in Chambers's *Dictionary*? That his mother was a fairy is more possible, since Chambers defines this 'imaginary human being' as of 'graceful form, capable of kindly or unkindly acts towards men: ... an enchantress: a creature of overpowering charm'. As to this last phrase, witness the only extant letter she wrote Carroll when visiting her sick father in Hull:

> My dearest Charles,
>
> I have used you ill in not having written to you sooner but I know you will forgive me. . . . All your notes have delighted me, my precious child, and show me you have not quite forgotten me. I am always thinking of you, and longing to have all round me again more than words can tell. . . . I hope my sweetest Will says

---

* Harold Bayley remarked in *Archaic England* that an etymological connection seems to exist between 'elf' and 'eleven'. It does indeed, because 'eleven' was originally 'one-leave', that is, the number you go on to when you leave ten behind; while 'elf' starts with el for alder, and also has 'leave' tacked on behind in its other meaning of 'life'. We may also note that 'alder', 'old' and 'aliment' have a common root.

The connection between eleven with lessons also has historical antecedents, because the reformation of the calendar in 1752 caused the anguished cry of 'Give us back our eleven days!' to be heard throughout England. As a result of the change, January 13 (Old Style) became known as January 1 (Circumcision Day), which in turn displaced March 25 (Lady's Day) as the start of the legal year. He who is appointed to read the Second Lesson on February 4, however, will come upon the eleventh hour in Matthew xx.

1–16.

'mama' sometimes, and that precious Tish has not forgotten. Give them and all my other treasures, including yourself, 1,000,000,000 kisses from me, with my most affectionate love . . .

A fairy quickly becomes involved here, since this letter leads to a contrary piece of evidence from Isa Bowman (p. 23):

> There! I have written 'a thousand pieces' and a thoughtless exaggeration of that sort was a thing that Lewis Carroll hated.

Isa Bowman (p. 26) then quotes one of Carroll's letters, written in the violet ink he always used at that time:

> My own Darling,
>     It's all very well for you and Nellie and Emsie to write in millions of hugs and kisses, but please consider the *time* it would occupy your poor old very busy Uncle! Try hugging and kissing Emsie for a minute by the watch, and I don't think you'll manage it more than 20 times a minute.

He took 'millions' to mean 2 million at least, and working out the sum involved he found it would mean 23 weeks of hard work. 'Really, my dear girl,' he ended, '*I cannot spare the time.*' We conclude from this that his mother must have been a fairy,* for the quantity of kisses she sent on that one occasion would have occupied each of her children for twenty years: and no mother would inflict such labour on a precious child unless she knew that a year of ordinary time only lasted a day by her reckoning.** Even so, he would have been justified in putting the old nursery rhyme into effect:

> Let's go to the wood, says this pig.
> What to do there? says that pig.
> To look for my mother, says this pig.
> What to do with her? says that pig.
> Kiss her to death, says this pig.

---

* Or perhaps a guardian angel. 'You say you don't see "how they can be guided aright by their dead mother, or how light can come from her". Many people believe that our friends in the other world can and do influence us in some way, and perhaps even "guide" us and give us light . . . My own feeling is, it *may* be so: but nothing has been revealed about it.' (Letter to Ethel—, quoted by Collingwood in *Life and Letters*, p. 209.) Carroll was sufficiently interested in this possibility to join the Society for Psychical Research soon after it was founded in 1882.

** But Carroll may have learnt an interesting lesson from this kind of reckoning, since when he grew up he called himself 'Uncle': which, of course, is slang for a pawnbroker.

We have another proof that Carroll came from fairy stock in the fact that he and all his brothers and sisters were named after relatives; for when the hero of 'Phantasmagoria' tried to put the Phantom in its place, he growled

> 'You're getting as familiar
> As if you were my cousin!'

continuing that that was a thing he would not stand, 'and so I tell you flat'.

These words have already come in handy when dealing with the Riddle, and when combined with the lateness of the hour when the Phantom appeared, they give us more clues as to what happens on the twelfth. It is the same thing that happens when you come round to the beginning again, as we may find by returning to the DIFFI-CULTY he proposed in 'The Rectory Umbrella': but instead of asking where, in its passage round the earth, the *day* changes its name and loses its identity, we shall ask this of clock time. We are entitled to do so by reason of Alice having said that the earth takes twenty-four hours to turn round on its axis ('"Talking of axes," said the Duchess, "chop off her head!"') – or is it twelve?

The answer is that clock time loses its identity at 12, which marks the end of one cycle and the beginning of another. At this hour the two hands are superimposed or, we could say, 'snarked'. The very word *snark* confirms this, being made up of a slow mover and a fast one, or rather, with Shakespeare's 'Devouring Time' in mind, one that breaks its fast, leaving you flat broke.

It may also break into your sleep. Our evidence for this comes from the *Alices*, which both have 12 chapters. True, Carroll dropped one chapter from *Looking-glass* largely on Tenniel's advice. But by this happy accident it was Chapter X that came to be titled 'Shaking' and Chapter XI, 'Waking' (these contain 59 and 8 words respectively, giving us the fine Nonsense total of 67), so that Alice can wake up out of 'Oh! such a nice dream' in Chapter XII, as the black kitten that was the Red Queen makes its reappearance known by purring. *Wonderland* ends in the same way, except that the awakening is not given a chapter to itself but an unnumbered epilogue. With this arrangement Nonsense can come full circle, to the end that those who 'engage with the Snark – every night after dark – / In a dreamy delirious fight' will always come to in the Boojum of waking reality.

But we need a clincher, which is to be found in the Advice from a Caterpillar.

> Alice remained looking thoughtfully at the mushroom for a minute, trying to make out which were the two sides of it; and, as it was perfectly round, she found this a very difficult question.

However, at last she stretched her arms round it as far as they would go, and broke off a bit of the edge with each hand.

Can we conclude anything from this episode but that Alice then set the mushroom at the half-way hour of six o'clock, where the Hatter was stranded?

That what happens on the twelfth has to do with clock time is irresistibly confirmed by the fact that Dean Liddell sneezed every day at 12 while working on his Lexicon; and that his children often teased him about it,

> 'Speak roughly to your little boy
> And beat him when he sneezes:
> He only does it to annoy
> Because he knows it teases.'

So what happens at 12, for a start, is that Liddell turns into little. What more? We must remember that the Phantom announced his presence to the man of 42★ by sneezing. It followed this up when

★ We may here note another numerological curiosity, via what Carroll called A Magic Number: 142857. This, treated as a circulating decimal, is the equivalent of $\frac{1}{7}$. One of its properties is that the other fractions of 7 are found by continually moving the first number to the back (e.g. .428571 = $\frac{3}{7}$). But the decimal point will move back one step if we take the sixty minute hour as unity and divide it by 42, for the result is 1.42857.

reciting his 'lesson in Biography' by asking for a pinch of snuff after it had mentioned the Double. This accords with tradition, for it has been the custom since antiquity to consider a sneeze as the motion of the Double or soul in the brain, which attests to the truth of whatever may then have been said. What happens at 12, then, is the Double, who is the twelfth child.

But what gets snuffed out? Certainly a baby does if there is too much pepper in the kitchen: it will then turn into its disreputable Double, the changeling. And what happens if this Double is snuffed out in its turn? Why, it will become a Phantom, the twelfth kind of family sprite.

> 'I've often spent ten pounds on stuff
>   In dressing as a Double;
> But, though it answers as a puff,
> It never has effect enough
>   To make it worth the trouble.'

## Chapter X

# A negative development

Alice herself had a narrow escape from being snuffed out after drinking from the little bottle labelled 'DRINK ME'. She then had the curious feeling of shutting up like a telescope, and so waited a moment to see what would happen: 'for it might end, you know, in my going out altogether, like a candle. I wonder what I should be like then?'

Let us now deal with this problem in the spirit of the Riddle, whose answer so far proves to be a draught that sticks in the throat. Of course, the contents of the bottle had 'a sort of mixed flavour of cherry-tart, custard, pineapple, roast turkey, toffee, and hot buttered toast', so it was not exactly a *black* draught. However, our guess is that Alice would have turned into a black *light* if she had gone out altogether, following a clue in 'The Walking Stick of Destiny': 'It is difficult to imagine what a black light looks like, but it may be obtained by pouring ink over a candle in a dark room.' Indeed, Alice nearly tried this very experiment on the White King when he was feeling faint, though by the time she had found a bottle of ink he had recovered and was reaching for his memorandum book.

Carroll had in fact been introduced to the mysteries of the dark-room in 1855, and his zeal for photography continued until 1880. During this period he took the portraits of his relatives and friends, and of many eminent persons; also of a great many young girls. At first he posed these in their ordinary clothes, then in fancy-dress and night-robes, and finally in nothing at all.★ 'Being photographed',

---

★ '"He has described the appearance of the thing exactly!" the Professor exclaimed with enthusiasm. "Black Light, and Nothing, look so extremely alike, at first sight, that I don't wonder he failed to distinguish them!"' (*Sylvie and Bruno Concluded*, Chapter XXI.)

said Alice, 'was a sobering and frightening experience. The reward was to be invited into his awesome and mysterious dark room.' ('Lewis Carroll as recalled by Alice'.) And there, according to Beatrice Hatch, 'you might stand by your friend's side . . . and watch him while he poured the contents of several strong-smelling bottles on to the glass picture of yourself that looked so funny with its black face.' (Quoted by Isa Bowman, p. 16.) The photographic likeness having been successfully recovered, it was then filed according to the girl's Christian name, with notes on her age; and by 1863 he had already collected 107 such 'memoranda', as he called them. By 1880 his files were bulging, and his pursuit had given rise to rumour and the disquiet of his acquaintances. He therefore abandoned it, and took to drawing the nude in the studio of one of his former girl friends who acted as chaperone.

The poser that Alice set us at the beginning of this chapter can therefore be answered by posing her as a sitter according to the rules of Nonsense. Just how familiar a procedure this is can be found by reading some of the pieces Carroll wrote on photography, the first only ten days after his introduction to the art. This was 'Photography Extraordinary' (1855), in which the artist found how to develop the ideas of the feeblest intellect when they were once received on properly prepared paper.

The machine being in position, and a mesmeric rapport established between the mind of the patient and the object glass, the young man was asked whether he wished to say anything; he feebly replied 'Nothing'. He was then asked what he was thinking of, and the answer, as before, was 'Nothing'. The artist on this pronounced him to be in a most satisfactory state, and at once commenced the operation.

It should surprise no one that the 'Nothing' occupying the mind of the youth appeared, when first developed, as milk-sop regrets over a disappointment in love. Dipped into various acids, these were further developed into an example of the Matter-of-Fact School: the hero was transformed into a horseman riding a nag worth £40 or so, which stumbled while he was dismissing his regrets and the girl in complacent verses and caused him to sustain fairly severe injuries. Finally the artist developed the surd to the highest possible degree, according to the Spasmodic or German School. The hero's brain was then set on fire, Nothingness became his destiny and nothing remained of him in the end but three drops of blood, two teeth and a stirrup. 'The young man was now recalled to consciousness, and shown the workings of his mind: he instantly fainted away.'

The Artist himself may also be left 'shaken, and sore, and stiff, and bruised', as in 'A Photographer's Day Out' (1860). His name here is Tubbs, and he remarks that Photographers are said to be a blind race at best, 'that we seldom admire, and never love'. He longs to break this delusion, if he could only find a young girl realising his ideal of beauty – 'above all, if her name should be – (why is it, I wonder, that I dote on the name Amelia more than any other word in the English language?) – '*

This beauty duly appears, and the bewitched Tubbs goes to the limit when asking her to sit for him: 'before the day is out, Miss Amelia, I hope to do myself the honour of coming to *you* for a negative.' For, as Carroll was to say later in a Double Acrostic,

> A flat and yet decided negative –
> Photographers love such.

So Miss Amelia took him at his word, turned him down flat, and added to his bruises by wilfully mistaking what he said about his heart for a request for some tart. His rival having cut him a slice, 'I swallowed my rage – and the tart.'

---

* Probably to honour the memory of George III, who was born on June 4 (the date of 'Novelty and Romancement', where the hero's name is Stubbs), was primarily responsible for the Boston Tea Party, the Declaration of Independence on July 4, and the loss of the American colonies; and whose reason finally gave way after the death of his favourite daughter Amelia.

Let us develop these last words. We first dip into 'The Legend of Scotland' (1856–60), in which a ghost is pictured on the wall by means of a thing 'more terrible than Woordes and of that which Men call Chimera'. (We may English this chimera as Gryphon, because of Carroll's explanation in *Wonderland*: '(If you don't know what a Gryphon is, look at the picture.)'*)

The ghost is that of a stiff and perky lady, who wished that some Painter might paint her picture. Finding their charges too high she settled for a photographer: but this artist broke her completely, for his pictures either took in her head but left out her feet, or took in her feet but left out her head – which, of course, turned her into a laughing-stock. All this, she said, happened in a stroke of Time, and though she only frowned when asked what this might be, we have another answer: for the man who saw her apparition did so at midnight, after having supped well on a Green Goose.

We next develop this situation and the Green Goose into *Wonderland*, where Alice is swallowing down her anger over something the Caterpillar has just said. She was about to leave when he called her back, and told her the secret of the mushroom he was sitting on. Now, had Alice taken a bite from the middle of the mushroom she might have fared as badly as the stiff and perky ghost. But as it

---

*Carroll recorded another way of picturing ghosts in the diary he wrote for Isa Bowman after her visit to Oxford in 1888:

The same day, Isa saw a curious book of pictures of ghosts. If you look hard at one for a minute, and then look at the ceiling, you see another ghost there: only, when you have a black one in the book, it is *white* on the ceiling: when it is green in the book, it is *pink* on the ceiling.

was, she ate the piece she had broken off with her right hand. It was her middle that then vanished, for she shut up like a telescope and her chin hit her foot: but at least both her extremities were in view.

We must now recall the patient to consciousness and show her the workings of her mind. The Duchess would have called this drawing a moral, for instance:

> '"Be what you would seem to be" – or, if you'd like it put more simply – "Never imagine yourself not to be otherwise than what it might appear to others that what you were or might have been was not otherwise than what you had been would have appeared to them to be otherwise."'

This can also be understood as a rule, namely, that when a person of good Nouryture swallows her anger she has been made to shut up. The remedy for this is to establish a mesmeric rapport and then develop the negative. The result of this contract appears after the Photographer's Day's work as

> PICTURE 4. – The three younger girls, as they would have appeared, if by any possibility a black dose could have been administered to each of them at the same moment, and the three tied together by the hair before the expression produced by the medicine had subsided from any of their faces.

We must not be misled by this: a black dose *had* been administered to all three at the same moment, via the silver nitrate whose anagrammatic Title Is Raven – whence, of course, the photographer's old admonition to watch the birdie so that he can make a memorandum of the sitter.

# THE

# T R A I N:

### A First-Class Magazine.

" VIRE- ACQUIRIT EUNDO."

## VOL I.—FROM JANUARY TO JUNE, 1856.

## LONDON:
### GROOMBRIDGE AND SONS, PATERNOSTER ROW.
#### MDCCCLVI.

[ *The Authors of Articles in* " THE TRAIN," *reserve to themselves the right of Translation.* ]

TITLE PAGE TO THE TRAIN, VOLUME I.

# Chapter XI

# Rails In Parallel

Let us reflect a moment. When it is 12 o'clock on this side of the looking-glass, it will be 12 o'clock on the other side; though tradition tells us that if it is midday here it will be midnight there. If we lived in a dark-room the difference might pass unnoticed, together with the possibility that mirror time goes backwards. But if we do not, then we may well ask if it is ever present time on *both* sides so that we can pass from one to the other.

'"Yes, my lady, change at Fayfield," were the next words I heard (oh that too obsequious Guard!), "next station but one."' The narrator is the author of *Sylvie and Bruno*, and he is carrying a book titled 'Diseases of the Heart'. The lady is Lady Muriel Orme, Sylvie's human counterpart, who is reading a book on Domestic Cookery. Both are going to Elvestone, where she becomes engaged to a Captain. This breaks the heart of the hero, a doctor, though it is mended when she breaks her previous engagement in his favour. And one of the results of this is that she can now see the inhabitants of Outland as clearly as does the narrator.

What was to be done? Had the fairy-life been merged in the real life? Or was Lady Muriel 'eerie' also, and thus able to enter into the fairy world with me? The words were on my lips ('I see an old friend of mine in the lane: if you don't know him, may I introduce you?') when the strangest thing of all happened: Lady Muriel spoke.

'I see an old friend of mine in the lane,' she said: 'if you don't know him, may I introduce you?'

Enter again, then, our old friend *The Dynamics of a Parti-cle*, to introduce 'the human element into the hitherto barren region of Mathematics. Who knows what germs of romance, hitherto unobserved, may not underlie the subject?'

## INTRODUCTION

It was a lovely Autumn evening, and the glorious effects of chromatic aberration were beginning to show themselves in the atmosphere as the earth revolved away from the great western luminary, when two lines might have been observed wending their weary way across a plane superficies. The elder of the two had by long practice acquired the art, so painful to young and impulsive loci, of lying evenly between his extreme points; but the younger, in her girlish impetuosity, was ever longing to diverge and become an hyperbola or some such romantic and boundless curve. They had lived and loved: fate and the intervening superficies had hitherto kept them asunder, but this was no longer to be: a line had intersected them, making the two interior angles together less than a right angle. It was a moment never to be forgotten, and as they journeyed on, a whisper thrilled along the superficies in isochronous waves of sound. 'Yes! We shall at length meet if continually produced!'

Before we make this journey ourselves we must enter a caveat. It comes from *A New Theory of Parallels*, when C. L. Dodgson is quarrelling with a Mr J. Walmsley: 'Mr. J. Walmsley has hardly realised, as yet, the *fearful* difficulty of persuading two lines, under any conceivable circumstances, to do such a thing as "meet".' It is true that Dodgson thought that the exactitude of a parallel should be gauged by a transversal crossing both lines, but what if these are railway lines seen in perspective? And how does this affect Euclid's 12th axiom?

Let us then buy a ticket to Elveston and see what happens. Isa Bowman (p. 37) sets the scene:

Before starting on a railway journey, for instance (and how delightful were railway journeys in the company of Lewis Carroll), he used to map out exactly every minute of the time we were to take on the way. The details of the journey completed, he would exactly calculate the amount of money that must be spent, and, in different partitions of the two purses that he carried, arrange the various sums that would be necessary for cabs, porters, newspapers, refreshments, and the other expenses of a journey. It was wonderful how much trouble he saved himself *en route* by thus making ready beforehand. Lewis Carroll was never driven half frantic on a station platform because he had to change a sovereign to buy a penny paper while the train was on the verge of starting. With him journeys were always comfortable.

To this we must add that Carroll was well supplied with games and puzzles to amuse his child friends, or to inveigle strange children with; that at his death six travelling ink-pots were found amongst his effects; and that he invented a travelling chess-set with the pieces pegged into holes in the board.

This said, let us go by train to the Third Square with Alice. First we hear the chorus of voices that reprimanded her, when she

kept the Guard waiting for the ticket she did not have, with the cry: 'Why, his time is worth a thousand pounds a minute!' Now, while everyone knows that Time is Money, only those who live in Elfland know that it can be banked. We have the Professor in *Sylvie and Bruno* to thank for this information, for he tells us that 'By a short and simple process – which I cannot explain to you – they store up the useless hours: and, on some *other* occasion, when they happen to *need* extra time, they get them out again.'

However, *we* can explain the process by paying attention to what happened to Alice next. For the Guard then looks at her, first through a telescope, then through a microscope, and lastly through an opera-glass, after which he tells her that she is travelling in the

wrong direction. This is yet another variant of the Lobster Quadrille, with the single view of the far away cancelled by that of the very near and very small, to become a constant through the binoculars. As for going in the wrong direction, a microscope demonstrates this by reversing the image: and what all this has to do with Time is told us by Humpty Dumpty: 'Now if you'd asked *my* advice, I'd have said "Leave off at seven" – but it's too late now.'

Alice could have done one of two things to stop it being too late. The first was to 'Change engines – ' as a hoarse voice said, soon after the Guard had left: but if the train was dancing the Lobster Quadrille, it must have done so already. The second, suggested by a gentleman dressed in white paper, was to 'take a return-ticket every time the train stops'. This sounds like a doctor's prescription, and it only made Alice – well, not angry, but impatient. For did not the Red Queen promise her that in the Eighth Square it would all be feasting and fun?

So let us change the subject. According to Rule 3, this is done by drawing a parallel: and having done so, the problem, as we said earlier, is to know when it is present time on both sides. We shall now find it geometrically, by drawing a transversal athwart the lines. Such a transversal in railway circles is known, of course, as a sleeper. The Nonsense proof of this is quite straightforward: all we need do is find two characters acting in parallel who have a sleeper between them. The Mad Tea-party provides the obvious set with the March Hare, the Hatter and the Dormouse, whose connection with Time we have quite sufficiently discussed. Before this there is the Caterpillar, who is about to become a sleeper or chrysalis so that it can turn into a Butterfly; and Carroll has it address Alice 'in a languid, sleepy voice' to remind us of the fact. The parallel lines he is between are, of course, the two sides of the mushroom. And then there is the little Bill sent in by the White Rabbit. True, Bill does not fall asleep, but he has been kicked so hard as to lose consciousness. This must amount to the same thing, since he is then looked after by two guinea-pigs. They are later

suppressed in court, which is not surprising: for if we turn them into shillings they add up to 42.*

Turning to *Looking-glass*, we have the Tweedle brothers being unpleasant to Alice when she is

in some alarm, at hearing something that sounded to her like the puffing of a large steam-engine in the wood near them, though she feared it was more likely a wild beast.

It was, of course, the Red King, snoring his head off so that Alice could spend her time on the other side of the looking-glass. And finally, our argument reaches its necessary inversion when Alice changes from being a Pawn into a Queen. She then, as it were, parallels herself: and at this moment what do we find but the Red and White Queens asleep with their heads on each of her shoulders.

All this proves that real time and dream time run in parallel as

---

*In Carroll's day, a guinea-pig was slang for a special juryman, who was paid a guinea for his service.

long as a sleeper is present. But can they be said to *meet*? This being a knotty problem, let us quote from

# A TANGLED TALE*
## KNOT I
## EXCELSIOR
### *Goblin, lead them up and down*

In this, two travellers might have been observed returning swiftly home, the younger of the two musing:

'We shall scarce be back by supper-time. Perchance mine host will roundly deny us all food!'
'He will chide our late return,' was the grave reply, 'and such a rebuke will be meet.'

So much for Domestic Cookery. But we still have 'Diseases of the Heart' to consult, which should tell us to trace the origin of the complaint back to childhood. We are then in the rectory garden at Croft, where Carroll laid out a railway using a wheelbarrow, a barrel and a small truck as the train. He was, of course, the ticket agent, and he also wrote out two sets of rules. One of them is called 'Love's Railway Guide', and Rule 1 is as follows:

All passengers when upset are requested to lie still until picked up – as it is requisite that at least 3 trains should go over them, to entitle them to the attention of the doctor and assistants.

How else could Carroll have acquired the sleepers for his track? And we may thus deduce that parallel lines do not *really* meet, though they may be connected as the result of an accident: the kind of accident that later brought Carroll into touch with the editor of *The Train* (a magazine first started in 1856) who insisted that he invent his *nom-de-plume*.

'Life,' asked Carroll, 'what is it but a dream?' To which we may now add, what is it but a railway train? To get a view of this, we start with a letter of 1852 that Carroll wrote while visiting his uncle Skeffington:

We had an observation of the moon and Jupiter last night, and afterwards live animalcules in his large microscope: this is a most interesting sight, as the creatures are most conveniently transparent, and you see all kinds of organs jumping about like a

---

* 'This Tale originally appeared as a serial in *The Monthly Packet* beginning in April 1880. The writer's intention was to embody in each Knot (like the medicine so dexterously, but so ineffectually, concealed in the jam of our early childhood) one or more mathematical questions ... for the amusement, and possible edification, of the fair readers of that magazine.'

# "Love's" Railway Guide —

| Trains leave. | I | II |
|---|---|---|
| Croft — | immediately after dinner | when the engine is rested. |
| Liverpool — | about 5 m after — | does not stop — |
| York — | about 3 p.m. — | 4 – 1 m p.m |
| Manchester — | 3 – 5 m – p.m | train left behind as the engine go to tea — |

Rule. I. All passengers when upset are requested to lie still until pickedup — as it is requisite that at least 3 trains should go over them, to entitle them to the attention of the doctor and assistants —

II. If a passenger comes up to a station after the train has passed the next (i.e. when it is about 100 m off) he may not run after it but must wait for the next.

III. When a passenger has no money and still wants to go by the train, he must stop at whatever station he happens to be at, and earn money — by making tea for the station master (who drinks it at all hours of the day and night) and grinding sand for the company (what use they make of it they are not bound to explain) —

complicated piece of machinery, and even the circulation of the blood. Everything goes at railway speed, so I suppose they must be some of those insects that only live a day or two, and try to make the most of it.

(Quoted in Florence Lennon, *Lewis Carroll*, 1947, p. 81)

We go from an animalcule to the Baby in *Wonderland* without a stop:

The poor little thing was snorting like a steam-engine when she caught it, and kept doubling itself up and straightening itself out again . . .

This was the baby whose sneeze, together with 'the shriek of the Gryphon and all the other queer noises, would change . . . to the confused clamour of the farmyard' when Alice woke up. On similar lines, Phyllis Greenacre has suggested in *Swift and Carroll* (1955) that the 'Boo' of the Boojum is the singular echo of the multiple squalling of the eight children born after Carroll. This is likely, for he referred to this noise in a poem celebrating the first anniversary of Rachel Daniel's birth:

> 'Oh pudgy podgy pup!
> Why *did* they wake you up?
> Those rude nocturnal yells
> Are *not* like silver bells:
> Nor ever would recall
> Sweet music's "dying fall".
> They rather bring to mind
> The bitter winter wind
> Through keyholes shrieking shrilly
> When nights are dark and chilly:
> Or like some dire duet
> Or quarrelsome quartette,
> Of cats who chant their joys
> With execrable noise,
> And murder Time and Tune
> To vex the patient Moon!'

This mischievous verse gives us the history of a man (or a Mouse) who hates ' – C and D' and from it we infer that a baby who starts life as a Puffing Billy brings with it draughts and the weather appropriate to old age. It must then turn into something like the Aged Aged Man

> '*Whose face was very like a crow,*
> *With eyes, like cinders, all aglow,*

*Who seemed distracted with his woe,*
*Who rocked his body to and fro,*
*And muttered mumblingly and low,*
*As if his mouth were full of dough,*
*Who snorted like a buffalo –*
*That summer evening long ago,*
*   A-sitting on a gate.'*

Here then is our railway train at the level-crossing of old age, cinders and all, and with yet another animal noise. Can we be certain of our identification? Is a buffalo really like a steam-engine? Yes, if we think of the Wild West, of Buffalo Bill and the Iron Horse: an association obliquely supported by the discovery in 1950 of some pieces of wood (together with a child's white glove and a left-hand shoe) under the nursery floorboards at Croft, on one of which Carroll had written in a boyish hand –

> And we'll wander through
> the wide world
> and chase the buffalo.

Our train of thought has afforded us the view of some curious transformations since it started, and we may thus halt for a while to commiserate with the Aged Aged Man's laborious and lengthy pursuits to earn his penurious living. Time is Money, as we noted, but he seems to have gone off the rails somewhere. Or was he dreaming of Snarks every night? If so, this would explain why you should threaten the Snark with a railway-share – because of the rolling-stock, which will awaken the sleeper.

The Snark being on the line, this is the moment to remember the caveat we entered on earlier, concerning the two lines – one older than the other – that isochronously whispered 'Yes! We shall at length meet if continually produced!' This is an illusion, as can be verified by an observer looking down the straight, for 'he will find that the converging lines forcibly suggest a vanishing point'.★ This augurs ill for a train, which must also vanish. It does so by turning into a ghost, as we shall now demonstrate. We start with the White Queen:

---

★This comes from *The New Belfry*, in which Tom Quad is likened to a railway station – as it also is in *The Three T's*:

PISCATOR.  But, Sir, I see no rails.
LUNATIC.   Patience, good Sir! For railing we look to the Public.
           The College doth but furnish sleepers.

163

Her screams were so exactly like the whistle of a steam-engine, that Alice had to hold both her hands over her ears.

Why, we must ask, is it proper for the White Queen rather than the Red Queen to scream in this way? The answer comes via 'The Walking Stick of Destiny', an early story from Carroll's family magazine 'Misch-Masch':

Then an Awful Form (1) was seen, dimly looming through the darkness: it prepared to speak, but a universal cry (2) of 'corkscrews!' resounded through the cave, and with a noiseless howl it vanished.
(1) The ghost of the departed scream.
(2) it rolled spirally through the cave.

This must be followed by two passages from 'Phantasmagoria'. The Phantom is explaining that to make a house habitable for such as he, it must be trimmed: and when asked what this means,

'. . . the loosening all the doors,'
The Ghost replied, and laughed:
'It means the drilling holes by scores
In all the skirting-boards and floors,
To make a thorough draught.'

To this example of gimbling we add his lesson in court etiquette:

'*The King must be addressed as "Sir".*
*This, from a simple courtier,*
*Is all the Laws require:*

*But, should you wish to do the thing*
*With out-and-out politeness,*
*Accost him as "My Goblin King!"*
*And always use, in answering,*
*The phrase, "Your Royal Whiteness . . . . . . !"'*

We can now deduce that the White Queen screams like the whistle of a steam-engine because she is a ghost on a well-trimmed board – the kind Carroll used to play chess on, in fact, when travelling by railway. But whose ghost is she?

That of the Crow, for a start, which left its footprints on the face of the Aged Aged Man: for after it comes like a cloud, along comes the White Queen, 'running wildly through the wood, with both arms stretched wide, as if she were flying . . .' Of course, the Crow is a Bishop in the chess game, and its move has alarmed the White Queen who then removes to another square. But that both should be flying suggests that together they constitute an Awful Form, as we may find confirmed in 'The Three Voices':

> 'Yet still before him as he flies
> One pallid form shall ever rise,
> And, bodying forth in glassy eyes
>
> 'The vision of a vanished good,
> Low peering through the tangled wood,
> Shall freeze the current of his blood.'

And as for this vanished good, we may hear its screams from the passengers upset by Love's Railway Train, as its bogies run over them on its remorseless passage to that Terminus where the Arrival platform is used only by the departed.

Our train of thought, its pistons working like a baby in a tantrum, has appropriately vanished on the wings of Time, in a black cloud and with a ghost-like scream. For we have arrived at Fayfield Junction, where Lady Muriel is saying:

> 'Rest, rest – ' she broke off with a silvery laugh. ' – perturbed Spirit!' I finished the sentence for her. 'Yes, that describes a railway traveller *exactly!*'

Elvestone is the last stop, which is the great Riddle. Shall we catch our connection? Yes, if the reader will follow the Red Queen's advice to 'Speak in French when you ca'n't think of the English for a thing.' It goes without saying that the *correspondance* will then appear on the writing-desk: but the raven has vanished, for it can only be read between the lines.

R.I.P.

*Doodles by Dean Liddell.*
'*He was very patient of tedious speakers, and would solace himself by taking out his gold pen, and after wiping it carefully on the sleeve of his gown (his invariable practice) would draw wondrous landscapes on the pink blotting paper which lay before him.*' *(H. L. Thompson.)*

# Chapter XII

# Some plain answers

... and here the conversation dropped, and the party sat silent for a minute, while Alice thought over all she could remember about ravens and writing-desks, which wasn't much.

We have come to the end of our argument, and we return to the Riddle not only for form's sake, as the March Hare might have said, but to tease the reader with some last oddities. Carroll himself was certainly teasing Alice in this passage, for if she knew *nothing* about ravens and writing-desks would not the Riddle have fallen *completely* flat?

So what might Alice have known about ravens, for a start? Well, that her father was the cousin of Sir Henry Liddell, raised to the peerage in 1855 as the third Baron Ravensworth, of Ravensworth Castle (originally Ravensholme), in the Chester ward of County Durham. About writing-desks? That her father worked at his Lexicon on just such a one as Carroll did, at which you stand rather than sit; and that the house he owned in Denbighshire, at which she often spent her holidays, was called 'Penmorfa'. And about the Riddle? Why, what does *that* rhyme with?

But even so the Riddle must have been all Greek to her, unless Carroll had once told her that he was born near Chester, County Cheshire; that there is another Ravensworth Castle in Yorkshire, hardly a dozen miles from his boyhood home at Croft; that his mother was the daughter of Charles Lutwidge of Holmrook, a few miles to the north of Ravenglass, Cumberland; and that Muncaster Castle at Ravenglass was owned by the Pennington family. (It still is.)

Croft is on the Tees. Croft is also a station on the Durham–Darlington–York railway, and by a curious chance it was none other than Sir Henry's father, Sir Thomas Liddell, who was the patron of George Stephenson, designer of the Rocket, and who feasted upwards of 500 notables at the opening of the line in 1827. His family had removed from Liddell Castle on the river Liddell (which means 'loud') – this forms the boundary between Cumberland and Roxburgh – to Newcastle, where they became proprietors of large coal-works. Hence, of course, Sir Thomas's interest in Stephenson. Sir Henry himself was a Tory M.P. for nearly thirty years, and in his spare time wrote such works as *The Wizard of the North* (1833); he may also be connected with a certain J.G.'s *The Devil's Visit to Ravensworth* (1837).

Dean Liddell was like Sir Henry in being of aristocratic bearing. His biographer H. L. Thompson tells us that he was also stern, always sparing of praise, had no small talk, that he was noted for 'his perfect self-control and his inflexible justice', and that he was much interested in drainage because of an outbreak of cholera at Westminster School when he was its headmaster.★ The following anecdote is the nearest thing to a joke that Thompson records of him:

> On one occasion Sir Henry Acland brought to Christ Church a learned German professor who was very anxious to have a sight of the famous writer of the Lexicon. On enquiring for him at the Deanery, they were told that he was in Christ Church meadow. . . . On asking a workman whether he had been seen there, 'Oh, yes,' said the man, 'he has just gone down the drain.'
>
> (*Henry George Liddell. A Memoir*, 1899, p. 196)

Thompson also says of the Dean that 'distaste for the attempt to solve matters insoluble was an abiding element in his character'. We shall therefore leave him underground★★ and pursue the Riddle from the river that bears his name to the river it flows into, the Esk. The name is common enough: it is cognate with the river names Exe and Axe, and it means 'water' in Celtic. But is it not curious that Ravenglass is also on a river Esk, and Whitby, a seaside town much frequented by Carroll for holidays, on a third?

---

★As such he may well have been called the Beak, which is also slang for a magistrate; and fittingly enough his wife's maiden name was Reeve, the name for a chief magistrate in Northumberland.

Since she was the talkative one – as may be found in 'The Blank Cheque' (1874), where she figures as 'Mrs Nivers' – while her husband was the silent lexicographer, Dean of Christ Church, and Vice-Chancellor of Oxford University from 1870 to 1874, who figures as 'John (I beg his pardon, "Mr. Nivers" I should say: but he was so constantly talked *of*, and *at*, by his better half, as "John", that his friends were apt to forget he had a surname at all)', we may rephrase the Riddle thus: Why is Lorina Reeve like Henry George Liddell?

Several answers are possible, and can be worked out either by consulting the definition of a Couple (see p. 61), which fits *this* couple to the manner born; or the Trial scene ('you never had *fits*, my dear, I think?'). But the simplest answer comes out of Mrs Nivers's mouth – 'As if *I* couldn't talk enough for him!' with 'him' translated into 'U'.

★★ But not without raising a memorial to him, on which should be inscribed the fact that he and Carroll died within four days of each other.

168

As for Whitby, this is 'Whit-by (in old Norse Hvitabyr, White-town)', as Dean Liddell remarked in a Commemoration Sermon preached on the Sunday after St Frideswide's Day, 1880. There is another Whitby twenty miles west of Daresbury, Carroll's birth-place in Cheshire; there is Whitley Bay to the north of Newcastle, Whitburn near Sunderland where his cousins Wilcox lived, and Whitehaven near St Bees Head to the north of Ravenglass. Names beginning with Whit or White are also common enough, as are those beginning with Raven: in addition to the two we have men-tioned there is Ravenscar to the south of Whitby, and Ravenstone-dale Fell between Croft and Holmrook.

But the Riddle is complete if we now find an r-, a d- and an -ing with similar geography. So we must castle our rook and fly by way of Ravensworth in Durham to Croft, in order to be in the North Riding of Yorkshire. Drawing on the Tees we turn this into Writing, with the help of the White town on the Esk. The Dee, which is a magic river, then flows underground to become the source of the Esk near Ravenglass, and with a flat Be-caws the Ordnance Survey answers the riddle of why a raven is like a writing-desk. The only letter not accounted for is the aspirate. We must therefore say that though the Riddle marries place-names according to the proportion: Dodgson is to Lutwidge as Carroll is to Liddell, the affair must remain hopeless.

If the reader thinks that this is mere nonsense, and that all we have done is to pick and choose from the plain facts of experience, we may convert him by drawing a parallel. Let us then put Jabber-wocky on the plane superficies as we have the Riddle.

We know that the first verse of Jabberwocky was written in Croft, and the remainder some years later while Carroll was staying with his cousins, the Misses Wilcox, at Whitby near Sunderland. As we have noted, the complete version is a parody of a poem by his cousin Menella Smedley. But we must point out that Sunderland is on the river Wear, and so is Penshaw: and that Penshaw is the home of the Lambtons and of the Lambton Worm.* Moreover, there was also a Worm a mile or two from Croft, at Sockburn, where the Tees encircles the manor on three sides as if by a sock of water. This Worm was killed in the fourteenth century by Sir John

---

*A *Worm* in Old English meant a snake or dragon. The Lambton Worm started life as something resembling a lamprey that grew to enormous size, ravaged the countryside and, when cut in half, merely grew together again. The Lambton heir killed it by donning a suit of armour covered in razors; but his victory was conditional on his killing the first creature he met after the deed. As this was his father, whom he refused to kill, the Lambton family has been under a curse ever since.

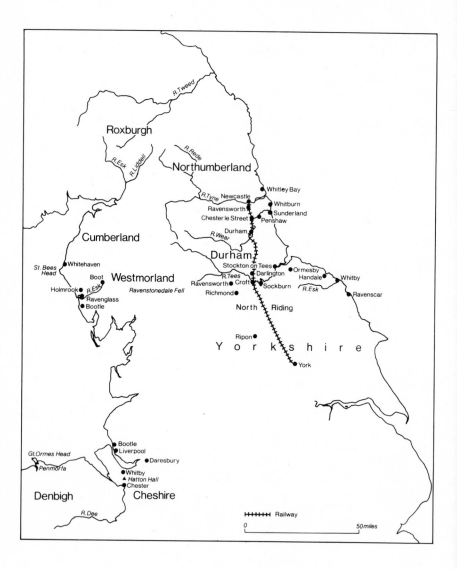

Roxburgh

*R.Tweed*

Northumberland

*R.Rede*

*R.Esk*
*R.Liddell*

*R.Tyne* Newcastle ● Whitley Bay
Ravensworth ● ● Whitburn
Chester le Street ● Sunderland
● Penshaw
Cumberland Durham
*R.Wear*
Durham

St.Bees ● Whitehaven Stockton on Tees ● Ormesby
Head ● Darlington Handale ● ● Whitby
Boot ● Westmorland *R.Tees* ● Croft
Holmrook ● *R.Esk* Ravensworth ● Sockburn *R.Esk* ● Ravenscar
● Ravenglass Richmond ●
● Bootle *Ravenstonedale Fell* North Riding

Y  o  r  k  s  h  i  r  e
Ripon ●
● York

Bootle
*Gt.Ormes Head* ● Liverpool
● Daresbury
*Penmorfa* ● Whitby
▲ Hatton Hall
Denbigh ● Chester

Cheshire

*R.Dee*

╫╫╫╫╫╫  Railway

0 ————————————— 50 miles

170

Conyers, and in succeeding generations the lord of the manor had the privilege of meeting all newly-appointed bishops of Durham on the bridge at Croft itself, and of presenting him with the sword that had done the deed. The custom was last observed in 1826, and the sword may now be seen in Durham Cathedral.

This is not all, for another legendary Worm lived at Handale,* a few miles from Whitby, while at Whitby itself St Hilda is credited with having rid Eskdale of snakes, by driving them over the cliff. Though *ask* or *asker* is the old name for a newt, we may take it that adders were the snakes concerned. These figure in the phrase 'mad [that is, angry] as an adder', later 'mad as a hatter'. (The madness of hatters was caused by the mercury used in felting hats. Mercury is also suspect for being the name of Tom Quad at Christ Church.) But the Worm itself, which is *ormr* in Old Norse, gives us Ormesby at the mouth of the Tees, and Great Orme's Head in Denbighshire, where 'Penmorfa' stands. The name also turns up in *Sylvie and Bruno* as that of the heroine, Lady Muriel Orme.

To sum up, we have found one Worm at Penshaw on the river Wear, and two others at Handale and Sockburn. Can Plain Superficiality go further in creating an appearance?

Oh yes: by taking a giant stride** from the Bootle that is five miles south of Ravenglass to the Bootle seventeen miles north-west of Daresbury. It is then but a step to Chester, leaving Hatton Hall just outside.

Chester, one of the main Roman stations in England, takes its name from Latin *castra*, a fortified camp. The word also gives us *castle*. Now, though a castle is a rook in chess, a rook is not a raven. In spite of appearances, however, it is worth castling a raven even if it means putting up a front before the wrong beak. For we then find ourselves on the forecastle of a ship, and about to be snarked.

---

*There was once a priory here, as can be found by reading the *Victoria County History*. By chance, the account of this priory is immediately followed by that of Keldholme: 'The patronage of this house passed from the Stutevilles to the Wakes, lords of Liddell, by the marriage in the early part of the 13th century of Joan, heiress of Nicholas of Stuteville, to Hugh Wake.' I have not been able to discover whether Hugh was any relation to Hereward, whom Morcar joined during the rebellion against the Conqueror, or how the Wakes had become lords of Liddell.

**If need be, with the help of Carroll's good friend Henry Kingsley. Born two years before Carroll, he published, a year before *Wonderland* was told, a novel called *Ravenshoe*. Lest there be any misunderstanding, this rhymes with 'toe', not with 'boo'.

"Alas! what boots——"

Milton's *Lycidas*. line 64.

As Carroll said in his Preface to the *Snark*, the poem contains noble teachings in Natural History. The one we finally need to extract concerns the Beaver whose Latin name, *castor*, suggests a relation to *castra*. This would have to be on the grounds that beavers build dams on rivers, in which they lodge. But Nonsense will be as interested in the beaver's tail, which is flattened into a scaly paddle sometimes known as its rudder. With this the inhabitant of the forecastle can steer the ship when the Boots is not acting as helmsman at the stern, and tells us why it was the Beaver who had often (the Bellman said) saved them from wreck, though none of the sailors knew how.★

This state of affairs will appear less improbable after considering the Beaver's habit of making lace in the bow. Would it have been chain lace, for the anchor? Point lace, if ever the crew had to go by train? Pillow lace, to solve problems on? Or, since most things in the *Snark* begin with a B, Brussels lace, Birmingham lace, bobbin lace? Or bride lace, to honour Alice in her anagrammatic form of 'Lacie'? Originally a technical term in lace-making, this later came to refer to sprigs of rosemary bound up for use at weddings, and then to a bonnet string. But as it is unlikely that the proper ingredients were present for its fabrication, we must conclude that the Beaver was indeed helping out the helmsman by making him a *boot-lace*.

---

★ But not always, perhaps, by using its rudder. For if the ship tended to gripe, a dose of castor oil would soon have made it move again. Had there been another Beaver aboard, of course, the ship could have run *on* castors.

These are not the only reasons for letting the Beaver make its appearance here. A beaver once meant a child's bib and, later, the vizor of a helmet. Thus, when Hamlet asked about his father's ghost, 'What, saw you not his face?' Horatio answered, 'Oh yes, my Lord, he wore his Beaver up.' After that, a beaver was a top hat made of beaver fur (just as *beavers* could be gloves of beaver fur), so that in Carroll's day 'In beaver' was university slang for being, as the *New English Dictionary* says, 'In a tall hat (and the costume which accompanies it) instead of cap and gown: in non-academical costume.'

With this, Plain Superficiality leads us directly back to Carroll. Picture him then as Alice did when he had made ready for a trip upon the river: he has changed his black clerical outfit for a white suit, his top hat for a straw one, but he is still wearing his black shoes and his black and grey cotton gloves.★ He is in the bows with a tale in his mouth, Canon Duckworth is rowing stroke, and Alice is sitting with her hand on the tiller between Edith and Lorina. The river is the Thames, which at Oxford is known as the Isis: 'and so best to avoid the onslaught of the ravenous alligators, which infest the banks on either side', as Carroll wrote in *The Three T's*, they are going safely down the middle, leaving a wake behind them and guided by a pun – '*In medio tutissimus Ibis*'. With this we may finally dispose of the writing-desk along with the raven, for the Egyptians held the Ibis to be the inventor of writing, and we have the Beaver to work away at this, and to lace the final draught with a quill.

A tangled tale? Yes: Knot X.

'It's hardly fair,' muttered Hugh, 'to give us such a jumble as this to work out!'

'Fair?' Clara echoed bitterly. 'Well!'

And to all my readers I can but repeat the last words of gentle Clara:

FARE-WELL!

---

★ Perhaps he will have taken with him some of the following items, which were auctioned off after his death: a watch, a chronometer, an English calendar clock with compensating balance, and a circulating time-piece; a pocket sundial-cum-compass; a thermo-barometer and two aneroids; three telescopes, two microscopes and three opera-glasses. But he will have left behind the one human skull he owned, together with the bones of one human hand and of one human foot, though whether they were right ones is not known.

173

A BOAT, beneath a sunny sky
Lingering onward dreamily
In an evening of July –

Children three that nestle near,
Eager eye and willing ear,
Pleased a simple tale to hear –

Long has paled that sunny sky:
Echoes fade and memories die:
Autumn frosts have slain July.

Still she haunts me, phantomwise.
Alice moving under skies
Never seen by waking eyes.

Children yet, the tale to hear,
Eager eye and willing ear,
Lovingly shall nestle near.

In a Wonderland they lie,
Dreaming as the days go by,
Dreaming as the summers die:

Ever drifting down the stream –
Lingering in the golden gleam –
Life, what is it but a dream?

# Tailpiece

The time has come to end this enquiry, in spite of the temptation to make some concluding remarks on, for instance, charge, and charm, and parity, on coincidence and quarks – and why black holes are double binds, and whether νοῦς needs σάρξ. But I really cannot afford to deal with these forms of the Higher Nonsense, for even if I had the capacity I fear the effort would land me with the kind of overdraft that made the Phantom sneeze, though he was only following his own calling:

'Long bills soon quenched the little thirst
   I had for being funny.
The setting-up is always worst:
Such heaps of things you need at first,
   One must be made of money!'

For the same reason I shall not attempt to give a bibliography of all the writings on Dodgson, and Carroll, and Nonsense of every kind, which I have read and profited from. I am well aware that this leaves me open to a charge of ingratitude, indeed, that I must now face the music of the Riddle on my own: for its last notes tell me that a raven is like a writing-desk because it bodes ill for owed bills.★ Having thus taken my medicine with a Spoonerism, I can at least try to mitigate its effects by appending a number of quotations dealing with the raven's natural and supernatural history. These will show the immemorial tradition that Nonsense is heir to, and will also corroborate the more unlikely parts of my argument. The writing-desk has proved difficult to do equal justice to, as will be seen; and as I have sufficiently dealt with the Hatter, who asked the Riddle, I end with a small anthology on his companion the Hare.

---

★ This brilliant turn of phrase is the invention of James Michie, to whom I once again stand indebted.

# The Raven

The raven breeds very early in the year, in England resorting to its nest, which is usually an ancient if not an ancestral structure, about the middle or towards the end of January. Therein are laid five to seven eggs ... and the young are hatched before the end of February.

(Encyclopaedia Britannica, 11th edition)

Mainly during breeding season, but to some extent at other times, performs remarkable evolutions in air, suddenly turning belly upwards and gliding thus for short distances or 'nose-diving' with closed wings.

(Witherby, Jourdain, Ticehurst and Tucker, Handbook of British Birds, 1945)

Of inspired birds, ravens were accounted the most prophetical. Accordingly, in the language of that district, to have the foresight of a raven, is to this day a proverbial expression, denoting a preternatural sagacity in predicting fortuitous events.

(The Reverend K. Macaulay, The Story of St. Kilda, 1794)

*Elijah, having prophesied against Ahab, is sent to Cherith*

And the ravens brought him bread and flesh in the morning, and bread and flesh in the evening; and he drank of the brook.

(I Kings xvii. 6)

Swainson supposed that the threat to naughty West Riding children, that a black raven would take them away, was a reminiscence of the period of the Norse raids. William the Conqueror is depicted on the Bayeux tapestry under a raven banner.

(E. A. Armstrong, The Folklore of Birds, 1958)

> If a raven cry just o'er his head
> Some in the town have lost their maidenhead.

(Brand, Popular Antiquities, 1905 edition)

Come: the croaking raven doth bellow for revenge.

(Shakespeare, Hamlet)

CORVUS was the Raven in Chaucer's time, and the Germans still have Rabe; but the French follow the Latins in Corbeau, as the Italians do in Corvo, and we in the Crow. It was a noted constellation with the Greeks and Romans, and always more or less associated with the Cup and with the Hydra, on whose body it rests. Ovid, narrating in his *Metamorphoses* the story of Coronis, and of her unfaithfulness to Apollo, said that when the bird reported to his master this unwelcome news he was changed from his former silver hue to the present black. This story gave rise to the stellar title Garrulus Proditor [the garrulous betrayer].

Another version of the legend appears in the *Fasti* – viz., that the bird, being sent with a cup for water, loitered at a fig-tree till the fruit became ripe, and then returned to the god with a water-snake in his claws and a lie in his mouth, alleging the snake to have been the cause of his delay. In punishment he was forever fixed in the sky with the Cup and the Snake; and, we may infer, doomed to everlasting thirst by the guardianship of the Hydra over the Cup and its contents. From all this came other poetical names for our Corvus – Avis Ficarius, the Fig-Bird; and Emansor, one who stays beyond his time.

. . . Nor is the reason for the association of Corvus with Hydra evident, although there is a Euphratean myth, from far back of classical days, making it one of the monster ravens of the brood of Tiamat that Hydra represented; and upon a tablet appears a title that may be for Corvus as the Great Storm Bird . . .

> (Abridged from R. H. Allen, *Star Names, Their Lore and Meaning*, 1899)

Roc, or more correctly RUKH, a fabulous bird of enormous size which carries off elephants to feed its young . . . In Indian legend the garuda on which Vishnu rides is the king of birds.

> (*Encyclopaedia Brittanica*, 11th edition)

rook, n. a castle in chess. [O.Fr. *roc* – Pers. *rukh*.]

> (*Chambers's Dictionary*)

When Viṣṇu is awake he rides upon a bird, half vulture, half man, named 'Wings of Speech' (Garuḍa).

Garuḍa is said to represent the hermetic utterances of the Vedas, the magic words on whose wings man can be transported from one world into another with the rapidity of light, the strength of lightning.

In the Purānic lore Garuḍa is a son of Vision (Kaśyapa) and She-before-whom-Knowledge-Bows (Vinatā).

She-before-whom-Knowledge-Bows quarrelled with her co-wife, Chalice-of-Immortality (Kadru), the mother of the 'ever-moving', the *nāgas* or serpents who are the cycles of time. From her Garuḍa inherited his hatred of serpents.

Garuḍa lives south of the Niṣada country near a gold-producing river in the Land-of-Gold (Hiraṇmaya). He is depicted as 'a bird immensely big and strong, equal in splendour to the god of fire'.

He was so brilliant that at his birth the gods worshipped him, taking him for Agni. Virile and lustful, he takes all the shapes he pleases. Terrifying as the sacrificial poker, his eyes are red and brilliant as lightning.

Once Garuḍa stole the ambrosia from the gods so as to purchase the freedom of his mother, who had been imprisoned by Chalice-of-Immortality, the mother of serpents. Indra, who discovered the theft, recovered the ambrosia from Garuḍa, deluding him through friendly overtures when he saw that the thunderbolt could not kill him and battle would not lead to success.

(Abridged from A. Daniélou, *Hindu Polytheism*, 1964)

Know also that our *rock* – veiled behind the figure of the dragon – first lets escape an obscure, stinking and venemous wave, whose smoke, thick and volatile, is extremely toxic. This water, whose symbol is the *raven* ('corbeau') cannot be washed and whitened except by fire. And this is what the philosophers let us understand when, in their enigmatic style, they recommend the artist to *cut its head off*.

The dog of Khorassan, or sulfur, draws its appellation from the Greek word *Korax*, equivalent to *corbeau*, vocable that again serves to designate a certain *blackish fish* about which, if we had permission, we would say some curious things.

Now, Cain signifies *acquisition*, and that which the artist acquires from the start is the *black and enraged dog* spoken of by the texts, the *corbeau*, first witness of the Magistery. It is also, according to the version of the Cosmopolite, the *fish without bones, échénéis*, or *remora* 'which swims in our philosophic sea'.

In the spoken language of the Adepts, however, this body is hardly designated otherwise than by the term 'violet', first flower to be seen born and opening by the sage, in the spring time of the Work, transforming its green bed into a new colour . . .

Noah, opening the window of the vessel, looses the *raven*, which is, for the alchemist and in his minuscule Genesis, the replica of the cimmerian shades, of those tenebrous clouds which accompany the hidden elaboration of new beings and of regenerated bodies.

(Fulcanelli, *Les Demeures Philosophales*, 1960, my translation)

> And thou treble-dated crow,
> That thy sable gender mak'st
> With the breath thou giv'st and tak'st,
> 'Mongst our mourners shalt thou go.
> (Shakespeare, 'The Phoenix and the Turtle')

This has been interpreted in three ways: that the bird, crow or raven, (i) changes its sex at will, which Grosart recorded as a still popular belief concerning the crow; (ii) conceives not 'by conjunction of male and female', but by 'a kind of billing at the mouth' (Swan's *Speculum Mundi*, 1635); (iii) conceives and lays its eggs at the bill (*Hortus Sanitatis*).

(Abridged from G. Wilson Knight, *The Mutual Flame*, 1966)


## The Writing-desk

And there came a writing to him from Elijah the prophet, saying, Thus saith the Lord God . . . Behold, with a great plague will the Lord smite thy people, and thy children, and thy wives, and all thy goods: And thou shalt have great sickness by disease of thy bowels, until thy bowels fall out by reason of the sickness day by day.

(II Chronicles XXI. 12–15)


And I went unto the angel, and said unto him, Give me the little book. And he said unto me, Take it, and eat it up; and it shall make thy belly bitter, but it shall be in thy mouth sweet as honey.

(Revelations X. 9)


The second way whereby bodies become black, is an Atramentous condition or mixture, that is a vitriolate or copperose quality conjoyning with a terrestrious and astringent humidity; for so is *Atramentum Scriptorium*, a writing Ink commonly made by copperose cast upon a decoction or infusion of galls. I say a vitriolous or copperose quality; for vitriol is the active or chief ingredient in Ink, and no other salt that I know will strike the colour with galls; neither Alom, Sal-gem, Nitre, nor Armoniack.

(Sir Thomas Browne, *Pseudodoxia Epidemica*, *The Sixth Book*, Chapter XII, edited by Charles Sayle, 1904)


*42nd Set of Concrete Propositions, proposed as Premisses for Sorites.*
(1)   There is no box of mine here that I dare open;
(2)   My writing-desk is made of rose-wood;
(3)   All my boxes are painted, except what are here;
(4)   There is no box of mine that I dare not open, unless it is full of live scorpions;
(5)   All my rose-wood boxes are unpainted.
Answer: My writing-desk is full of live scorpions.

(Lewis Carroll, *Symbolic Logic*, 1895)   179

# The Hare

LEPUS, the Hare, is located just below Orion and westward from his Hound. The Denderah planisphere has in its place a Serpent apparently attacked by some bird of prey; and Persian zodiacs imitated this.

Aelian, of our 2d century, referred to the early belief that the hare detested the voice of the raven, – a belief that has generally been put among the zoölogical fables of antiquity; but Thompson suggests for it an astronomical explanation, as 'the constellation Lepus sets soon after the rising of Corvus'.

(Abridged from Allen, *Star Names, Their Lore and Meaning*)

Xenophon says 'When he is awake he shuts his eyes, but when he sleeps his eyelids remain open though his eyes do not move.'

Gubernatis adds; 'The moon is the watcher of the sky, that is to say, she sleeps with her eyes open; and so is the hare, hence the *somnus leporinus* became a proverb.'

(J. W. Layard, *The Lady of the Hare*, 1944)

In China, as in India, the hare is said to inhabit the moon. I know of no legend of how it got there similar to the Indian legend of its self-immolation in fire and its subsequent translation by the god into the moon, but the miraculous healing element in the Indian story is replaced in China by the belief that the hare lives in the moon eternally compounding the elixir of life.

(Layard, ibid.)

. . . the Norwegian custom that the man who is thus said to 'kill the hare' must give 'hare's blood' in the form of brandy to his fellows to drink.

This rite calls to mind the celebrated 'black broth' of the Spartans which was made of the blood and bowels of a hare.

(Layard, ibid.)

Many people, if they meet a hare when going to work, will return home, and not venture out again until the next meal has been eaten.

(Billson, quoted in Layard, ibid.)

Better known than the hare's use as an omen is its notorious role as one of the 'familiar' animals into which witches transformed themselves when prosecuting their alleged nefarious designs.

Thus we are all familiar with the superstition of turning over the silver in our pocket when seeing the new moon, in order to render the moon favourable to us, in the same way that we are taught as children to utter the word 'hares' or 'rabbits' on the first day of each new month. It is, therefore, interesting to read Frazer's statement that 'the only way to make sure of hitting a witch animal is to put a silver sixpence or a silver button in your gun' . . . quite clearly due to the kind of symbolism which speaks of 'paying a man out in his own coin'.

(Layard, ibid.)

> But come! Cain with his thorn-bush strides the sill
> Of the two hemispheres; his lantern now
> Already dips to the waves below Seville;
>
> And yesterday the moon was full, as thou
> Should well remember . . .
>
> (Dante, *Inferno*, Canto XX, translated by D. L. Sayers)

Or else one must come in with a bush of thorns and a lanthorn and say, he comes to disfigure, or to present the person of moonshine.

(Shakespeare, A Midsummer Night's Dream)

The man i' the moon's too slow.

(Shakespeare, The Tempest)

The love-chase is, unexpectedly, the basis of the Coventry legend of Lady Godiva. The clue is provided by a miserere-seat in Coventry Cathedral . . . which shows what the guide-books call 'a figure emblematic of lechery' . . . If [all the facts] are combined into a picture, the 'figure emblematic of lechery' has a black face, long hair, a raven flying overhead, a hare running ahead, a hound at her side, a fruit to her lips, a net over her and a goat under her. She will now easily be recognised as the May-eve aspect of the Love-and-Death goddess Freya, *alias* Frigg, Holda, Held, Hilde, Goda, or Ostara.

(Robert Graves, The White Goddess, 1961)

The double sex of single Hares, or that every Hare is both male and female, beside the vulgar opinion, was the affirmative of *Archelaus*, of *Plutarch*, *Philostratus* and many more. . . . Now therefore although we deny not these several mutations, and do allow that Hares may exchange their sex, yet this we conceive doth come to pass but sometimes, and not in that vicissitude or annual alteration as is presumed . . . For besides the inconceivable mutation of temper, which should yearly alternate the sex, this is injurious unto the order of nature . . . Now the grounds that begat, or much promoted the opinion of a double sex in Hares, might be some little bags or tumours, at first glance representing stones or Testicles, to be found in both sexes about the parts of generation; . . . But to speak properly, these are no Testicles or parts official to generation, but glandulous substances that seem to hold the nature of Emunctories.

For herein may be perceived slender perforations, at which may be expressed a black and faeculent matter. If therefore from these we shall conceive ammixtion of sexes in Hares, with fairer reason we may conclude it in Bevers . . .

The last foundation was Retromingency or pissing backwards; for men observing both sexes to urine backward, or aversly between their legs, they might conceive there was a foeminine part in both; wherein they are deceived by the ignorance of the just and proper site of the Pizzel . . . which in the Hare holds not the common position, but is aversly seated, and in its distention enclines unto the Coccix or Scut. Now from the nature of this position, there ensueth a necessity of Retrocopulation . . .

(Sir Thomas Browne, *Pseudodoxia Epidemica, The Third Book,*
Chapter XVII, edited by Charles Sayle, 1904)

# List of Illustrations

# Index

pig, guinea-, 159
pigs fly, when, 65
pillow lace, 172
Pillow Problems, 48, 70, 85, 86, 95, 128
pink, 82, 120, 152
pity, 61, 82, 84
pixy, 143
Plain Superficiality, 23, 39, 41, 42, 128, 171, 173
plane superficies, 156, 169
Poe, Edgar Allen, 22, 62
poet, 96, 97, 98, 100, 118
poetic faculty, 52, 58
poetic logic, 137
poetry, 54, 64, 71
point, 23, 35, 46, 47, 57, 61, 62, 85, 128, 156
poison, 104, 105, 106, 141
poker, 73, 77, 140, 177
police, 66, 98
poltergeist, 143
porcupine, 138
portmanteau, 66, 67, 70, 71, 73, 75, 88, 117, 121, 122, 126, 131, 132
Postulates, 23, 24
Price, Bartholomew, 73, 132
Prickett, Miss, 124
prison, 44, 45, 77, 82, 83, 98, 118
Professor, 9, 91, 138, 140, 149, 157
pros, 64
prose, 64, 70, 97, 98
psychoanalysis, 12, 50
pudding, 73, 109, 139
pun, 7, 8, 39, 54, 70, 89, 136, 173
punch, 97, 98
punishment, 83, 96, 97
purple, 107
purr, 31, 146
purse, 122, 156
put-on, 21
put on shoes, 118
put to vote, 64

q, 52, 56, 59, 93
qu-, 33, 59
quadrille: see also Lobster Quadrille, 40, 41, 121, 125, 128
quarrels, 57, 81, 84, 85, 106, 108, 110
quartette, 162
Queen of Hearts, 36, 64, 80, 116, 142
Queens: see also Red and White Queens, 80
query, 57, 68

quill, 139, 175

r, 37, 40, 52, 55, 57, 58, 59, 62, 70, 100, 101, 112
Rabbit, White, 28, 57, 62
rabies, 34, 74
railing, 163
rails, 163
railway, 156, 160, 162, 163, 164
railway-share, 163
rath, 65, 69, 70, 72, 73, 135
raven, 21, 26, 28, 31, 37, 38, 40, 41, 42, 49, 54, 62, 64, 65, 74, 108, 110, 126, 128, 141, 153, 165, 167, 169, 171, 175–8, 179
Ravenglass, 28, 167, 168, 169, 171
ravenous, 41, 56, 61, 65, 107, 138, 173
Ravenshoe, 171
Ravensworth, 167, 168, 169
raving, 37, 39, 40, 42, 51, 110, 139
read, 31, 39, 41, 62, 165
reading, 42, 51
reason, 87, 88
red, 39, 62, 95, 110, 117, 129
Red King, 42, 159
Red Queen, 80, 97, 108, 146, 159, 164, 165
reeling, 51
Reeve, Lorina, 168
reflex, 139, 140
Resurrection, the, 82, 85, 132
retort, 39, 50, 74, 107
return ticket, 131, 158
revenge, 101
reversal, 70
reverse, 34, 37, 40, 62, 86, 88, 126, 158
revolution, 47, 64, 67, 97
revolutionary instrument, 61, 67
rheumatism and lumbago, 78, 91, 140
rhyme, 52, 167
rich, 74, 112
Richard III, 136
Richard de Hoghton, Sir, 96
riddle, 7, 9, 21, 22, 37, 38, 41, 44, 45, 46, 49, 58, 62, 71, 78, 112, 113
Riddle, 7, 9, 12, 21, 23, 30, 33, 37, 38, 39, 41, 42, 46, 47, 51, 54, 55, 57, 59, 62, 64, 74, 85, 102, 107, 112, 122, 128, 139, 146, 149, 165, 168, 169, 175
Riding, North, 169
Riemann, 88

Rieu, E. V., 22
right, 51, 74
right ear, 77, 78
right eye, 78
right foot, 77, 141
right hand, 54, 153
right-hand foot, 76, 77, 78, 121, 125
right-hand shoe, 125
Right Witness, 43
Rilchiam, 70, 97
R.I.P., 155, 165
rivals, 58, 61, 66, 67, 83, 87, 101, 102
Rocket, 167
romance, 8, 11, 12, 81, 156
Romance languages, 59
romancement, 73
rook, 28, 84, 169, 171
rote, 51
rudder, 24, 31, 47, 48, 96, 117, 172
ruddy, 110
rude, 37, 38, 39, 40, 42, 59, 74, 75, 94, 162
Rule 1, 35, 36, 45, 95
Rule 2, 35
Rule 3, 35, 41, 47, 158
Rule 4, 35
Rule 5, 35, 38, 41, 128
Rule 6, 38
Rule 7, 39
Rule 8, 45
Rule 9, 45, 46, 47, 96
Rule 10, 48
Rule 11, 50
Rule 12, 50, 83
Rule 13, 50
Rule 14, 70, 71, 117
Rule 15, 74
Rule 16, 85
Rule 17, 85
Rule 18, 85, 87, 108
Rule 19, 87, 89, 114, 121, 123, 129
Rule 20, 90, 123, 128, 129
Rule 42, 39, 90, 91, 94, 117, 129
Rule of 3, 122
Russell, L. J., 94
R. W. G., 126

s, 31, 52, 100
sad, 115, 117, 138
Sakalya, 45–6, 47
Salmon, George, 85
school, 39, 61, 67
scorpions, 179
Scott-Giles, C. W., 135
scr-, 56, 59, 69
scratch, 56, 61, 62, 72, 74, 80